BI Without the BS

BI Without the BS

*Real-World Strategies for
Better Requirements*

Eva Polini
Karina Ghozali

BEP

BUSINESS EXPERT PRESS
Leader in applied, concise business books

BI Without the BS:
Real-World Strategies for Better Requirements

Copyright © Business Expert Press, LLC, 2026.

Cover design by Eva Polini and Muhammad Arslan

Interior design by S4Carlisle Publishing Services, Chennai, India

First published in 2026 by
Business Expert Press, LLC
222 East 46th Street, New York, NY 10017
www.businessexpertpress.com

ISBN-13: 978-1-63742-920-4 (paperback)
ISBN-13: 978-1-63742-921-1 (e-book)

Portfolio and Project Management Collection

First edition: 2026

10 9 8 7 6 5 4 3 2 1

EU SAFETY REPRESENTATIVE
Mare Nostrum Group B.V.
Mauritskade 21D
1091 GC Amsterdam
The Netherlands
gpsr@mare-nostrum.co.uk

Dedication

To Anne-Marie, Vincent, and Avélye

Description

Most people understand the value that business intelligence (BI) projects can deliver. However, effective capture of requirements still poses a challenge for many in the profession, often resulting in rework and late delivery of solutions, along with increasing costs.

This book challenges the common belief that it is just a matter of asking stakeholders what they want or need, which can prove difficult, especially when many stakeholders are unsure of what that is.

Industry experts Eva Polini and Karina Ghozali provide valuable and practical guidelines for gathering requirements for BI projects using simple, accessible language that addresses the following:

- Basics of business analysis domain
- Business analysis applied to BI
- Empower business analysts beyond their job scope

After reading this book, you will have the information you need to deliver BI assets that will be widely adopted and delivered on time and budget with minimal errors and rework, allowing you to establish credibility with your stakeholders and peers.

This book is perfect for BI or data visualization specialists/managers, business analysts, project managers, and others involved in managing or implementing BI solutions. It is created with years of practical experience across telecommunications, banking, retail, and IT industries around the world.

Contents

List of Figures

Preface

Both of us have worked in the business intelligence (BI) space for a combined 25 years and in that time we have seen many examples of BI projects that fall apart completely or elements of it had to be redone because requirements were not captured properly in the beginning.

We were inspired to take our learnings and put it together in one book to guide others on how to effectively gather requirements for a BI project.

People often overlook this step or deem it as not important, only to face problems along the way that could have been easily avoided. This often results in spending lots of time, money, and resources reiterating or having to start all over again.

This book can be used by project managers, business analysts, analysts or others who are involved in managing or implementing a BI solution. This will prevent you from wasting time, money and resources unnecessarily.

The journey is a rewarding experience as it provides step-by-step guidance on how to effectively gather requirements for BI projects of all levels of complexity. Whether you are starting from scratch or creating new features, the book aims to help you create relevant and timely products and reduce product defects.

Different techniques will be discussed on how to collect information and when to use them. The book also highlights what you need to watch out for when using these techniques.

There are tips on how to streamline communications so that everyone is on the same page, enabling you to take stakeholders and team members on a journey and work toward the same goals. This ultimately leads to better user experience and the attainment of company goals.

Acknowledgments

My first debt is to Karina, my coauthor. Without her experience and her engagement nothing would have been possible. Thanks for being an amazing coworker, friend, and coauthor.

My heartfelt appreciation goes to my partner in crime, Vincent Diallo-Nort—thanks for supporting my projects and forcing me to be a better version of us.

"Mamie" for being an undetectable support in ups and downs since I'm.

Moune and my late Pou for teaching to seek adventures and challenges.

I extend a special thanks to Hugo, Patrick Maulaz, and Paula Vieira Eskinazi: Their eyes mean a lot to me.

A long life debt to Colette Rolland and Selmin Nurcan, my teachers.

—Eva

I would like to extend my heartfelt thanks to Eva for inspiring me to embark on this journey of writing this book with you. Your guidance, mentorship, and friendship have been invaluable, and you truly are one of a kind.

This book would never have come to fruition without the support and interactions of countless individuals. To everyone who has helped, shaped, challenged, and refined my thoughts along the way, I cannot express my gratitude enough.

I also want to extend special thanks to my family for their unwavering support and encouragement, and to my parents for continually motivating us to pursue excellence in all our endeavors.

—Karina

This success couldn't be turned into reality without our proofreaders: Anne-Marie Lecerf, Michael Gumbley, Vincent Diallo-Nort, Chris Christodoulou, Flo Auquier.

Thanks Nigel Wyatt, Scott Isenberg, and Business Expert Press and Delvin Fletcher for believing in this project and for their dedication and their professionalism. Thanks also to ENI for being the earliest believer.

Finally, thanks to Sean, Michael, Susan, Jakob, Paul, Maxime, and the current MSC team for inspiring us to improve my BI and leadership skills.

—Us

Foreword

Convergence.

It's such an important concept in the technology-driven world we all live in. And yet its opposite—divergence—so often seems to be what we are presented with and the way we are encouraged to think if we're not careful.

Choose my software over your software. My method is better than your method. My technology makes your technology obsolete. My approach is the key to success! You must do this or not do this. And on and on the narratives go. And we wonder why implementations fail.

And leaders are frustrated.

Eva Polini and Karina Ghozali challenge us to a convergent mindset in this book, born out of their years of experience in BI initiatives. But they aren't suggesting that methods don't matter. Quite the opposite. They matter a lot. And doing successful work requires a broad and deep understanding of method.

They challenge us to learn and think comprehensively about models, approaches, needs, tools, and both the advantages and limitations that they bring to the specific context of BI work.

And they challenge us to keep learning, always. That's one of my learnings from reading this book. To never assume that I have it all figured out. To realize that there are many options for me to consider. But also to understand that at a certain point I need to stop research and start doing! And that's where this convergence idea returns to such importance.

It's how I bring methods and frameworks and tools together that matters. Convergence challenges me to really understand context, purpose, value, and outcome in my work as I approach the crafting of BI solutions. It challenges me to weigh different approaches and tools and methods from a posture of understanding so that I can apply them, or choose from among them, or maybe combine them in a way that is best suited for my current challenge. Sometimes, I am building on the last work that I finished. Sometimes, I am taking a new approach. Sometimes, I am creating new combinations for this situation. But my foundation is built on defining objectives, identifying key results, modeling business events, clarifying business concepts, and grounding them in operational data.

I know this book can help you. I encourage you to read it quickly, then read it slowly, then mark it up—with notes from your work or highlights to come back to later or ideas that are new that you need to think about further. And then put it to work, in your work.

—Delvin Fletcher
President and CEO
International Institute of Business Analysis

CHAPTER 1

Introduction

This book offers an in-depth examination of the convergence between business analysis, business intelligence (BI), and data domains. It is designed to provide insights, frameworks, and methodologies that enhance the understanding of how business analysis principles can be utilized in BI and data projects, promoting effective decision making and successful outcomes.

Scope and Structure of the Book

The content is organized into three distinct sections, each building upon the previous to create a cohesive narrative that aligns foundational knowledge with advanced applications and strategic considerations.

Foundations of Business Analysis

The first section establishes the fundamental principles and practices of business analysis. It introduces essential concepts and frameworks that underpin effective analysis in any business context. Key topics include:

- Key Concepts in Business Analysis: Definitions, core principles, and foundational frameworks
- The Decision-Making Process: The role of business analysis in guiding strategic and operational decisions
- Costs and Risks of Poor Business Analysis: An examination of the consequences of inadequate or poorly executed analysis
- Challenging Misconceptions: Addressing prevalent misunderstandings and presenting strategies to challenge the status quo

- Analogies for Clarity: The use of relatable comparisons to facilitate meaningful discussions
- Types of Requirements: An exploration of functional, nonfunctional, and other categories of requirements

Business Analysis in BI and Data Domains

Building on the foundational principles, the second section focuses on the application of business analysis in the context of BI and data initiatives. This section bridges the gap between theory and practice, emphasizing techniques and approaches specific to these domains. Key areas of focus include:

- Techniques for BI and Data Projects: A detailed exploration of workshops, interviews, brainstorming, design thinking, and other methodologies tailored to the BI and data context
- Modeling for BI: The use of modeling languages, such as Unified Modeling Language (UML), to represent organizational objectives, workflows, and data processes
- Data-Specific Requirements: Critical aspects such as security, data quality, governance, architecture, and data modeling

Running BI Portfolio Beyond Business Analysis

The final section extends the discussion beyond the core domain of business analysis, addressing the strategic and operational elements of managing BI initiatives. This section aims to equip professionals with tools and frameworks for effective implementation and governance. Topics include:

- Requirements and Project Management: Integration of requirements management within various project methodologies
- BI Maturity Frameworks: Tools and frameworks for evaluating the maturity of organizational BI capabilities
- Developing a BI Strategy: A structured, step-by-step approach to formulating an effective strategy
- Innovative BI Governance: Methods and approaches to maximize the impact of governance in BI initiatives

Purpose and Intended Outcomes

This book aims to provide a detailed and structured approach to understanding and applying business analysis within the BI and data domains. By integrating theoretical foundations with practical applications, it offers a resource for navigating the complexities of BI initiatives while fostering strategic alignment and value generation.

Through the structured presentation of concepts, methodologies, and case studies, the book enables the exploration of innovative approaches to business analysis and BI. The content is designed to be both a theoretical foundation and a practical guide, supporting the effective implementation of BI initiatives in diverse organizational contexts.

CHAPTER 2

Basics of Business Analysis

Global Organizations

When working in the field of BI, business analysis, or requirements engineering (RE), professionals often refer to industry standards and certifications established by well-known organizations. Among them, three major institutions stand out: IEEE (Institute of Electrical and Electronics Engineers), IIBA (International Institute of Business Analysis), and IREB (International Requirements Engineering Board). Each of these organizations plays a significant role in structuring best practices, methodologies, and professional development in their respective domains.

Institute of Electrical and Electronics Engineers

What Is IEEE?

The IEEE is a global organization dedicated to advancing technology for the benefit of humanity. It is one of the largest technical professional organizations in the world, with members spanning across various disciplines such as electrical engineering, computer science, and BI.

IEEE's Role in BI and Data Management

The IEEE sets widely accepted standards, research publications, and best practices for technological and engineering advancements, including data governance, artificial intelligence (AI), and business analytics. Some key IEEE contributions relevant to BI include:

- IEEE 830-1998: Recommended practices for software requirements specifications (useful for BI requirement gathering)

- IEEE Big Data Initiative: Focuses on best practices for data processing, analytics, and machine learning models
- IEEE P7000 Standards: Guidelines for ethical AI, critical in BI and predictive analytics

International Institute of Business Analysis

What Is IIBA?

The IIBA is a leading global association for business analysis professionals. It provides internationally recognized frameworks, best practices, and certifications that help analysts deliver value-driven solutions to businesses.

IIBA's Role in BI

The IIBA primarily focuses on business analysis methodologies and frameworks that apply to BI projects. The Business Analysis Body of Knowledge (BABOK Guide), published by the IIBA, is one of the most recognized standards for business analysis and includes key insights into data-driven decision making.

International Requirements Engineering Board

What Is IREB?

The IREB is an independent organization that focuses on RE standards and best practices. The IREB is responsible for defining frameworks that improve the quality and structure of requirements in software and data projects.

IREB's Role in BI

While the IREB does not specifically focus on BI, it plays a critical role in ensuring BI requirements are well defined, structured, and validated before development begins. The most relevant IREB framework is the

Certified Professional for Requirements Engineering (CPRE), which follows structured methods to elicit, document, and manage requirements.

Conclusion

Each of these organizations brings a unique perspective to BI project management and data governance. While the IEEE contributes to technological advancements and standards, the IIBA focuses on business analysis methodologies, and the IREB ensures that RE is structured and properly implemented. For BI professionals, leveraging these frameworks and certifications can significantly enhance the quality, efficiency, and long-term success of BI initiatives.

Key Concepts and Business Analysis

Understanding the terminology in business analysis and RE is crucial for effective communication and project success. Below are definitions of key terms—Business Analysis, Design, and Requirement—as provided by the IREB and the IIBA, along with a comparison between Design and Requirement.

Business Analysis

- IIBA Definition: Business Analysis is the practice of enabling change in an organizational context by defining needs and recommending solutions that deliver value to stakeholders.
- IREB Definition: While the IREB does not provide a specific definition for Business Analysis in the available glossary, it focuses on RE, which involves eliciting, documenting, validating, and managing requirements.

Both the IIBA and the IREB emphasize understanding stakeholder needs and defining solutions. The IIBA provides a broader scope, encompassing the entire practice of enabling organizational change, whereas the IREB concentrates on the requirements aspect within that practice.

Requirement

- IIBA Definition: A requirement is a usable representation of a need. Requirements focus on understanding what kind of value could be delivered if a need is fulfilled.
- IREB Definition: A requirement is a need that is perceived by a stakeholder or a capability or property that a system must have to achieve stakeholder objectives. It can also be a documented representation of a need, capability, or property.
- IEEE Definition:
  According to the Institute of Electrical and Electronic Engineers (IEEE), a requirement is defined as:

"(1) A condition or capability needed by a user to solve a problem or achieve an objective.

(2) A condition or capability that must be met or possessed by a system or system component to satisfy a contract, standard, specification, or other formally imposed document.

A documented representation of a condition or capability as in (1) or (2)."

Together, these definitions highlight the dual nature of requirements: representing stakeholder needs and providing system-level specifications to fulfill those needs. This comprehensive approach ensures alignment between business objectives and technical solutions, facilitating clarity and effectiveness throughout the RE process.

Design

- IIBA Definition: Design is a usable representation of a solution. It focuses on understanding how value might be realized by a solution if it is built.
- IREB Definition: Design refers to a plan or drawing produced to show how something will look, function, or be structured before it is made. In software product development, it distinguishes between creative design, which shapes the look and feel of the

product, and technical design (also called software design), which determines the inner structure of the product, particularly the software architecture.

Both definitions recognize design as a representation of a solution. The IREB differentiates between creative and technical design, emphasizing both the external appearance and internal structure. The IIBA focuses on the usability and value realization aspects of the design.

Decision Process

The Decision-Making Process

BI plays a critical role in supporting decision-making processes by enabling access to centralized, homogeneous, and historical data. Unlike operational systems, which focus on real-time access to individual records or small datasets to support operational tasks, BI systems are optimized to handle mass queries targeting significant volumes of data.

The decision-making process itself can take various forms, from fully automated solutions to decisions based on intuition or collective input. Regardless of the form, the underlying structure of decision making remains consistent. While certain steps may be emphasized or omitted depending on the context, the iterative nature of decision making ensures continuous refinement and improvement.

The decision-making process is iterative, consisting of eight key steps. These steps form a cycle, where evaluation of the results can trigger a new iteration. Below is an overview of the decision-making cycle (Figure 2.1):

- Understand the Situation
- Define the Problem and Compile the Data
- Diagnose the Problem
- Define the Objectives
- Develop Alternatives
- Select the Solution
- Implement the Solution
- Evaluate the Results

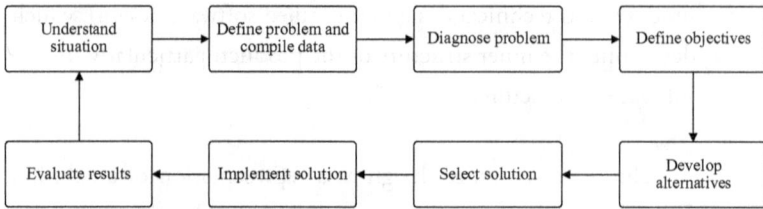

Figure 2.1 Decision-making process

Detailed Breakdown of the Decision-Making Process

Understand the Situation

This foundational phase involves identifying the context and nature of the issue. By the conclusion of this step, the decision maker develops a preliminary understanding of the situation and identifies areas requiring further investigation.

Define the Problem and Compile the Data

The decision maker collects relevant data to verify that the problem exists and assesses its significance. Contextual data ensures the problem is not only real but also actionable.

Diagnose the Problem

At this stage, the decision maker gathers data to confirm the existence of the problem and contextualize its impact and main drivers. This step ensures that the problem is clearly defined, along with its boundaries and impact, laying the foundation for effective solutions.

Define the Objectives

Objectives are clarified by defining what success looks like. Specific key performance indicators (KPIs) are established, serving as benchmarks for evaluating outcomes and guide the evaluation process. The desired outcome is articulated.

Develop Alternatives

Various solutions are explored, with each option analyzed for its advantages, disadvantages, and potential consequences. This stage ensures a well-rounded understanding of possible courses of action.

Select the Solution

The most suitable solution is chosen based on its alignment with objectives, overall feasibility, and anticipated risk and impact (advantages and consequences).

Implement the Solution

The selected solution is executed to resolve the problem. Effective implementation requires coordination, monitoring, and adaptation as necessary.

Evaluate the Results

The solution's effectiveness is measured against the initial objectives using the predefined KPIs. If results fall short of expectations, the process loops back to the earlier stages, starting a new iteration with refined insights.

Why Is Requirement Management So Important?

RE is the structured process of defining, documenting, and maintaining the requirements of a system. As one of the most critical stages in the systems engineering and software development life cycle, it lays the foundation for the entire development process. When adapted to BI solutions, RE becomes indispensable, ensuring the success and adoption of these systems. While the fundamental process remains consistent, certain steps may be emphasized or omitted based on the specific context of a BI project.

The primary objective of RE is to ensure that the final product aligns with stakeholder needs and expectations, while being delivered on time and within budget. The process involves actively engaging relevant stakeholders and team members to gather input and create a comprehensive set of well-defined requirements. These requirements serve as a blueprint, guiding the development process toward achieving project objectives.

This chapter explores the significance of managing requirements in the context of BI. It navigates the unique challenges of BI projects, addresses common roadblocks, and examines associated costs, risks, and misconceptions. By delving into these aspects, the chapter highlights how robust requirements management can drive project success and mitigate potential failures.

To develop a successful BI solution that will be adopted and effectively used, it is essential to first understand the various needs (question, problem) it aims to address. A well-designed BI solution supports these needs while outlining the features that must be developed. Requirements management plays a pivotal role in ensuring the solution aligns with stakeholder expectations and provides the desired outcomes.

In requirements management, there are eight key steps that serve as the foundation for achieving project and product success:

1. Elicitation: Gathering input from stakeholders to identify and document their needs
2. Modelization: Structuring and visualizing requirements to enhance understanding and communication
3. Specification: Detailing requirements clearly and unambiguously for use throughout the development process
4. Prioritization: Determining the most critical requirements to focus resources effectively
5. Dependencies Management: Identifying and managing relationships between requirements to prevent conflicts
6. Impact Analysis: Assessing the potential effects of changes to requirements on the project
7. Negotiation: Aligning requirements with stakeholder priorities while addressing constraints
8. Quality Control of Requirements: Ensuring requirements are complete, consistent, and traceable

A well-known proverb states, "Understanding the question properly is half the solution." This wisdom underscores the importance of exploring various approaches to achieving the same goal. This book provides guidance on finding the optimal approach before starting development to ensure the solution meets its intended purpose.

The Critical Role of Requirements Management in Project Success

From a project management, business analysis, and return on investment (ROI) perspective, RE plays a pivotal role in determining a project's success or failure. It serves as the foundation for aligning business needs with technical execution, ensuring that resources are effectively allocated, risks are minimized, and the final solution delivers measurable value.

From the RE Perspective

Research consistently underscores the vital impact of RE on project success. The Chaos Report (1995) found that 42 percent of a project's success is linked to effective requirements management, while 43 percent of failures stem from deficiencies in this area. More recently, the same group produced and enhanced version as part of the SMART Project (2014) reinforced these findings, identifying clear requirements, user involvement, realistic expectations, and a well-defined vision as key success factors.

Conversely, challenges such as lack of user input, incomplete requirements, and unrealistic expectations contribute to up to 48 percent of project difficulties. Inadequate requirements management is responsible for 52 percent of project failures, often due to scope creep, misalignment with stakeholder needs, and evolving project priorities. Additionally, research by Olson (2005) and Al Neimat (2005) highlights poor planning, dependency mismanagement, and shifting priorities as major risks leading to project failure (Figures 2.4).

From the Project Management Perspective

Project Management Institute's (PMI) Pulse of the Profession Report (2014) confirms the impact of requirements mismanagement, with

Project Success Factors

- ■ User Involvement 15.9 %
- ▦ Executive Management Support 13.9 %
- ■ Clear Statement of Requirements 13.0%
- ☐ Proper Planning, 9.6 %
- ■ Realistic Expectations 8.2%
- ☐ Smaller Project Milestones 7.7%
- ☐ Competent Staff 7.2%
- ☐ Ownership, Clear Vision & Objectives, Hard Working, Focused staff, Others 24.5%

(Pie chart values: 15,9%, 13,9%, 13,0%, 9,6%, 8,2%, 7,7%, 7,2%, 24,5%)

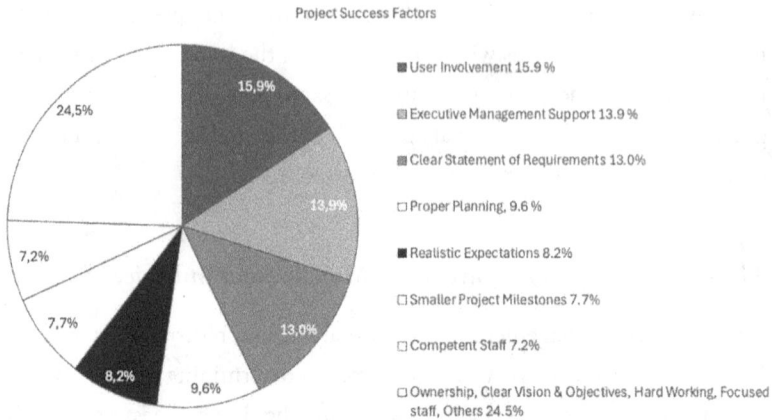

Figure 2.2 Project success factors according to SMART study 2014

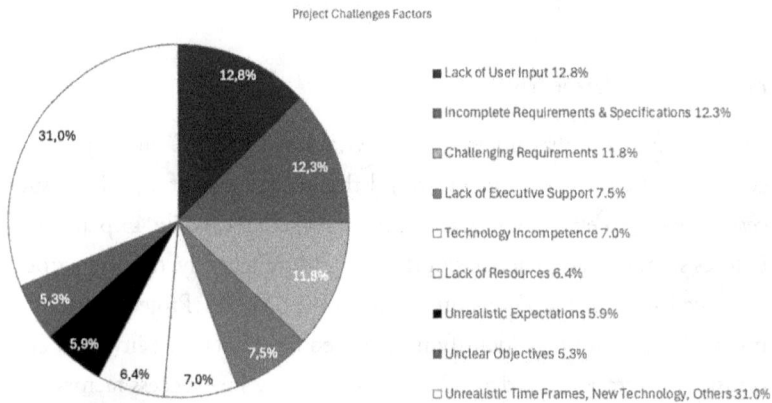

Project Challenges Factors

- ■ Lack of User Input 12.8%
- ■ Incomplete Requirements & Specifications 12.3%
- ▦ Challenging Requirements 11.8%
- ■ Lack of Executive Support 7.5%
- ☐ Technology Incompetence 7.0%
- ☐ Lack of Resources 6.4%
- ■ Unrealistic Expectations 5.9%
- ■ Unclear Objectives 5.3%
- ☐ Unrealistic Time Frames, New Technology, Others 31.0%

(Pie chart values: 12,8%, 12,3%, 11,8%, 7,5%, 7,0%, 6,4%, 5,9%, 5,3%, 31,0%)

Figure 2.3 Project challenges factors according to SMART study 2014

inaccurate requirements gathering (39 percent) ranking as one of the primary causes of failure, alongside organizational changes (41 percent) and shifting project objectives (36 percent). Meanwhile, the Standish Group Survey highlights user involvement, management support, and clear requirements as the top success factors for high-performing projects.

Ensuring ROI Through Effective Requirements Management

Regardless of perspective, well-defined requirements are a cornerstone of project success. They ensure solutions align with user needs, improving adoption and maximizing ROI. By fostering clarity, alignment, and

Project Failures Factors

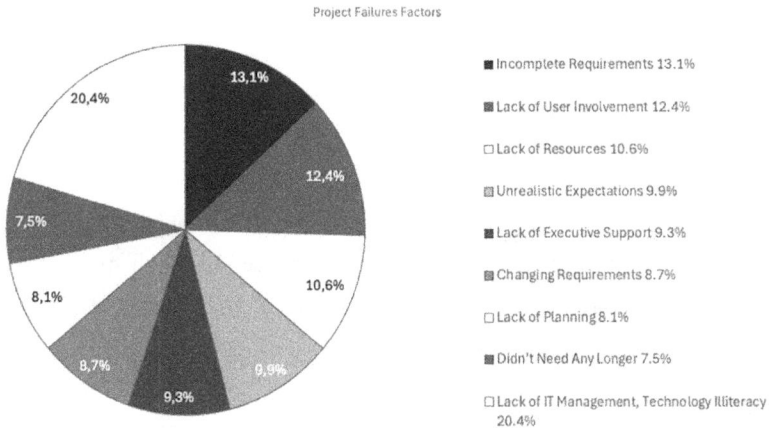

- ■ Incomplete Requirements 13.1%
- ■ Lack of User Involvement 12.4%
- □ Lack of Resources 10.6%
- ▨ Unrealistic Expectations 9.9%
- ■ Lack of Executive Support 9.3%
- ▨ Changing Requirements 8.7%
- □ Lack of Planning 8.1%
- ■ Didn't Need Any Longer 7.5%
- □ Lack of IT Management, Technology Illiteracy 20.4%

Figure 2.4 Project failure factors according to SMART study 2014

communication, strong requirements management mitigates risks, reduces costs, and enhances project outcomes, ultimately driving long-term business value.

Costs and Risks

This chapter explores the risks associated with poor or nonexistent requirements management. Such risks arise when the requirements process is not well structured, when requirements are ambiguous, or when the process is entirely overlooked. These shortcomings can lead to a variety of costs that affect the project itself, the delivered solution, and the users who rely on it. In this section, risks are addressed as potential future costs.

Project Costs

The costs of addressing issues in software development increase exponentially as a project progresses. According to a study by Boehm and Papaccio (1988), the cost of fixing a defect grows significantly depending on the project phase.

To illustrate:

- Fixing a defect in the requirements definition phase costs $1.
- In the design phase, the cost rises to $5.

- During the development phase, the cost increases to $10.
- In the testing phase, the cost jumps to $20.
- Finally, fixing a defect during the production phase can cost as much as $200.

This exponential growth highlights the importance of identifying and addressing defects early in the requirements phase. Although specific figures may vary, studies consistently show that the ratio of cost escalation remains stable over time.

Cost Overruns and Tight Deadlines

Organizations often place the requirements-gathering process at risk by imposing tight deadlines or prioritizing quick results. This pressure frequently leads to shortcuts, such as skipping requirements management and testing, which can compromise the reliability of the final solution. Such decisions increase the likelihood of bugs and project failures.

As the saying goes: "If you don't have time to do something right, you won't have time to fix it later." A poorly designed solution will require repeated patching, including bug fixes, upgrades, integration testing, and nonregression checks. These additional tasks can cause significant delays, making it difficult to meet deadlines while maintaining quality and usability. When time and budget are constrained, it is often more effective to reduce project scope rather than deliver poorly implemented features.

Demotivation and Loss of Confidence

Incomplete requirements can demotivate both end-users and technical teams. When needs are not adequately captured, users are less likely to adopt the solution, making change management and training efforts more costly and challenging. Additionally, in the long run, users may lose trust in the development team's ability to deliver effective solutions.

From the technical perspective, ambiguous requirements can lead to frustration among developers. Frequent changes or unclear objectives may give the impression that their work is undervalued or misaligned with stakeholder needs. This can result in reduced productivity, lower quality output, and increased maintenance challenges. On average, developers spend 60 percent of their time correcting bugs and errors—a figure that rises dramatically when systems are poorly designed or overly complex.

Stakeholder Costs

For nontechnical stakeholders, the costs and risks associated with poor requirements management are often difficult to quantify but can be significant. These impacts may affect functional stakeholders, end-users, clients, organizational beneficiaries, or even the broader community. The magnitude of these costs depends on the type and scale of the impact and decisions supported by the solution. It can be discomfort, productivity loss but also market loss.

Costs to the Business

Inadequate requirements can lead to business costs such as limited access to critical information or information of poor quality. Issues with data quality, refresh frequency, availability, or granularity can result in reduced productivity, discomfort for users, or even financial losses in the marketplace.

Cost of Training

When a solution fails to meet user needs or is overly complex, training costs increase significantly. Without adequate training, users may struggle to adopt the solution or use it incorrectly, further compounding inefficiencies and errors.

Cost of Developing Workarounds

In cases where a BI solution only partially addresses business needs, users often resort to creating workarounds, such as exporting data to Excel for further analysis. These workarounds, though sometimes necessary, introduce additional costs in terms of time and effort. They are rarely documented, unsustainable, and may lead to inconsistencies or inefficiencies across the organization.

Costs to Business Relationships

When stakeholder needs are not adequately addressed, frustrations can arise, leading to strained relationships. Stakeholders may feel unheard or undervalued, resulting in reduced cooperation and productivity. Over time, this lack of trust can negatively impact project outcomes and organizational collaboration.

Costs to Corporate Brand and Reputation

Poor requirements management can damage an organization's brand and reputation. For instance, if a BI solution publishes incorrect or misleading data, decision makers may act on inaccurate information. This can erode trust among customers, clients, and stakeholders, potentially leading to long-term reputational harm.

Cost of Breaching Legislation

Failing to meet legal or regulatory requirements can have severe consequences. If a company provides inaccurate or untimely data to customers or regulatory agencies, it may face penalties such as fines, audits, loss of commercial licenses, or even business closure. In extreme cases, board members may face legal action, including incarceration.

Cost of Uncertainty

The cost of uncertainty applies to all industries; but in some inadequate requirements management can have life-or-death consequences. Poorly defined requirements may result in insufficient data for decision making, preventing the identification of risks or the implementation of mitigation plans. This is particularly critical in sectors such as public health, laboratory research, and climate risk management, where the cost of uncertainty is measured not only in financial terms but also in human lives.

Conclusion

The costs and risks associated with poor requirements management extend beyond the immediate project scope, affecting stakeholders, business operations, and even organizational reputation. By investing in robust requirements management practices, organizations can reduce costs, mitigate risks, and ensure the delivery of effective and sustainable solutions.

Common BI Requirement Misconceptions

This section addresses common misconceptions that can hinder progress and prevent the adoption of better practices in daily operations.

Misconception 1: "Users Change Their Minds"

Variations of this idea often include statements such as: "Stakeholders don't know what they want" or "They don't even understand their own needs." It is essential to recognize that while stakeholders are experts in their domain, they may not have expertise in designing solutions.

A useful analogy can be drawn from Steve Jobs' approach to the iPhone. When developing the product, he didn't rely on future customers to define its functionalities and capabilities. Similarly, it is often challenging for users to articulate the specific features and capabilities of a future solution.

Moreover, there are legitimate reasons why business stakeholders might change their minds. Changes in organizational strategy, leadership, or market conditions can drive updates to operational processes, technical systems, and BI assets. These shifts are not necessarily signs of indecision but rather reflections of an evolving business environment.

Misconception 2: "It's Okay to Not Deliver by the Deadline"

Deadlines play a critical role in helping team members align toward a shared goal and maintain the project's trajectory. They are typically set based on organizational priorities, which in turn reflect the impact of the project on the business and its stakeholders. While challenges often arise during the project life cycle that can lead to delays, it is essential to identify the root causes of such delays and implement strategies to prevent or better manage them in the future.

Some projects are inherently complex, with goals that might initially seem unattainable. A compelling example of overcoming such challenges is the Rosetta mission and its attempt to land on the comet 67P/Churyumov-Gerasimenko. This story, led by the European Space Agency (ESA), represents a monumental achievement despite its ambitious goals and the immense obstacles faced.

In 1993, a team of scientists approached the European Commission to seek approval and funding for their vision. Their objective: to send a spacecraft to land on a comet, collect samples, and study its composition. What made this project particularly extraordinary was the scale of its ambition. The comet, roughly 3.5 by 4 km in size, was traveling at an incredible speed of 135,000 km/h and rotating on its axis every 2.4 hours. Furthermore, the mission's timeline stretched across decades, with a projected rendezvous in 2014, requiring the spacecraft to travel 650 million km from Earth.

When asked how such a mission would be accomplished, the team admitted that much of the required technology did not yet exist. Their plan relied on developing entirely new systems and bringing together 500 engineers from 50 companies across 14 countries. The complexity of the task demanded both innovation and collaboration on an unprecedented scale.

Despite its challenges, the mission succeeded in delivering a space probe after 21 years. The Rosetta spacecraft orbited the comet, and its lander, Philae, made contact with the comet's surface. While the landing was not perfect—Philae bounced due to the unknown surface composition—the mission achieved its primary scientific objectives. It remains a testament to international collaboration, of a highly complex project delivered on time. It's possible!

While not all projects require the same level of risk or ambition and cash, the Rosetta mission serves as a powerful reminder to aim high and embrace innovative approaches. Deadlines should not be viewed as arbitrary constraints but as opportunities to strive for excellence and push boundaries. As Norman Vincent Peale said: "Shoot for the moon. Even if you miss, you'll land among the stars."

Misconception 3: "All the Requirements Need to Be Written Down"

The process of gathering requirements should not become a burdensome and overly time-consuming activity. Requirements should only be documented when there is a clear need for them. When such documentation is necessary, the benefits often far outweigh the effort. Accurate and well-written requirements reduce the time spent maintaining the solution and provide a single, reliable source of truth for the team, minimizing the likelihood of duplication or misunderstandings.

Documenting requirements helps solidify the project's expectations and objectives, ensuring all stakeholders have a clear and shared understanding of what needs to be achieved. This documentation serves as a common reference point, aligning everyone involved. However, the level of documentation required depends on the project's complexity, scale, and stakeholder needs. Striking a balance is crucial—enough documentation to ensure clarity without overwhelming stakeholders with unnecessary details.

A Lesson from a Fable

Consider the following story:

"An engineer, an experimental physicist, a theoretical physicist, and a philosopher are walking through the Scottish Highlands when they spot a black sheep.

- The engineer exclaims, 'Look, the sheep in Scotland are black!'
- The experimental physicist corrects, 'Some of the sheep in Scotland are black.'
- The theoretical physicist chuckles and adds, 'Actually, at least one sheep in Scotland is black.'
- Finally, the philosopher, examining a nearby flower, looks up and says, 'On one side, anyway.'"

This metaphor illustrates how different perspectives can result in varying interpretations of the same observation. As Gérard Szymanski noted in *The Metaphor: Royal Way to Communicate*, effective communication requires acknowledging and addressing these differences in interpretation to ensure shared understanding. Writing down requirements can play a critical role in aligning perspectives, but it is not always necessary to formalize every detail.

Finding the Right Balance

Writing volumes of requirements does not guarantee project success, just as avoiding documentation entirely does not ensure failure. Success lies in ensuring all stakeholders have a shared understanding of the objectives and expectations—or, at the very least, recognizing and addressing differences. As with the metaphor of the black sheep, alignment among stakeholders is the key.

While telepathy might seem like the most efficient way to communicate business requirements, it is unfortunately not an option. Communication, with all its imperfections, remains our primary tool. Between what one person thinks, what they say, what another hears, and what they interpret, there are numerous opportunities for the message to be distorted. Documentation can help minimize these distortions by providing a reference point that stakeholders can revisit when needed.

When to Document Requirements

Requirements do not always need to be written down, but documenting them can serve as a valuable tool to:

- Align expectations among stakeholders.
- Provide clarity on complex or critical information.
- Serve as a reference to minimize miscommunication over time.

However, writing down requirements is not a guarantee of project or solution success. Instead, the focus should be on ensuring that communication is effective and that all parties have a common under-standing, regardless of the method used. The goal is not exhaustive docu-mentation but clarity, collaboration, and shared understanding.

Misconception 4: "There Is Only One Way to Gather Requirements"

There is no single "best" way to gather requirements for a BI project. Various methods and approaches have proven effective, but the choice depends on the specific context of the project, the people involved, their level of expertise, and the available data.

Requirements gathering is fundamentally a social activity, built on communication and collaboration. There are no magic formulas, step-by-step tutorials, or guaranteed tricks to make it work perfectly every time. Success relies on tailoring the approach to the unique circumstances of the project.

Choosing the Right Approach

The optimal approach for gathering requirements will depend on several factors. While the following list is not exhaustive, it highlights key criteria to consider:

1. Complexity and Criticality of the Needs:
   For example, gathering requirements for a legal compliance project will demand a different level of precision than estimating a five-year commercial forecast.
2. Type of Needs:
   The method for collecting requirements will vary based on the na-ture of the project—whether it involves implementing a technical platform, managing data security, or designing a visually appealing user interface.
3. Environment and Culture:
   Cultural factors such as individualism versus collectivism, power dynamics, gender roles, orientation toward long-term or short-term goals, and attitudes toward risk can all influence the

requirements-gathering process. For instance, an introverted environment may require a different communication strategy compared to an extroverted one.

4. Business Context:
   Elements such as project stress levels, visibility, and prior relationships between stakeholders can significantly affect the process. Stakeholders may come to the table with preconceptions or misconceptions, and part of the requirements-gathering process will involve addressing and resolving these to foster effective collaboration.

Requirements gathering is not a one-size-fits-all process. Success depends on understanding the project's unique characteristics and adapting the approach accordingly. By doing so, teams can create an environment that fosters open communication and ensures that all stakeholders' needs are accurately captured.

Misconception 5: "There's No Need to Define Requirements Because We Are Using Agile"

Regardless of the project methodology, it is essential to understand what needs to be developed and why. Just as it doesn't matter what vehicle you use—you still need to know your destination—projects require clarity on objectives, even in Agile environments.

Agile methodologies emphasize iterations, often allowing development to proceed without fully analyzing requirements under the assumption that issues can be addressed in subsequent iterations. However, this approach can lead to unnecessary rework and inefficiencies.

We challenge this mindset: why 'fail' or accept inefficiencies when they can be avoided? Defining requirements accurately, even in Agile projects, helps prevent avoidable setbacks, conserving time, effort, and resources. Iterations are an opportunity to refine and improve, but they should not be used as an excuse to skip the critical step of understanding and defining the project's goals from the outset and loop in circles.

Different Types of Needs

Various organizations, such as the IIBA, the IREB, and the IEEE, have developed structured approaches for managing requirements. Each of these organizations provides frameworks and best practices to define, document, and manage requirements effectively. While their methodologies may differ, they all aim to improve communication between stakeholders and ensure that business and technical teams are aligned.

To build a strong foundation in requirement classification, this chapter will first explore the definitions and principles established by these leading institutions. However, understanding requirements doesn't have to be limited to formal methodologies and technical jargon. To make these concepts more accessible, we will introduce two engaging analogies that illustrate the different types of needs in a relatable and practical way.

The first analogy, "Cold, Jumper, and Wool," helps clarify how different types of needs can be categorized and highlights the information necessary to address them effectively. This approach is particularly useful for business analysts, developers, and stakeholders, as it provides a structured framework for classifying and managing requirements.

The second analogy compares a BI project to running a restaurant. This perspective focuses on the granularity of requirements and how detailed they need to be. Just as running a restaurant involves balancing high-level business goals with operational details, BI projects must navigate different levels of requirement precision. By framing these discussions in familiar terms, this analogy simplifies communication with nontechnical stakeholders and enhances collaboration.

Through these comparisons, we will bridge the gap between formal requirement management methodologies and practical, real-world understanding. This approach ensures that all stakeholders—whether business-oriented or technical—can align on expectations and work together effectively to achieve project success.

Requirement Classification

One of the traditional methods for classifying needs involves separating them into functional and technical requirements. In this classification the word "requirement" is used as a definition of the solution, not of the goal/ problem to be solved.

- Functional requirements describe what the business needs the solution to accomplish. For example, the solution should allow users to download reports directly onto their laptops.
- Technical requirements specify how the functional requirements will be implemented, along with any associated constraints. For instance, reports should be downloadable in secured ".pdf" format.

A lesser-known but equally important classification comes from the Edward et al. (2000) model, which highlights the different types of needs across strategic, tactical, and operational levels. Understanding this classification can help address many of the challenges projects encounter.

Project Management Overview

Before a project begins or a BI solution is chosen, organizations typically define long-term objectives (e.g., market share targets or profitability goals) and the high-level strategies to achieve them. These strategies often revolve around product offerings, pricing, and target demographics, and are adapted over time to align with competitive and technological changes.

As the project starts, two additional types of needs emerge:

1. Product Needs: These relate to the solution being created. Teams will define the overall architecture, ensure components are integrated rather than siloed, and set priorities for component delivery.
2. Project Needs: These pertain to organizing and managing the project itself. Key considerations include selecting a project management methodology (e.g., Agile, Waterfall, or hybrid approaches), assembling a team, and setting quality expectations.

Tools for Capturing and Modeling Needs

Various tools and graphical representations can be employed to capture and model these needs effectively:

- Goal Trees to document business objectives and prioritize actions
- Process Models to outline operational structures and workflows
- Prototypes to illustrate functional needs and how the solution will support business processes
- Architectural Schemas to visualize technical and enterprise architecture, often supplemented with data models to detail data organization and workflows

The functional stakeholders typically define the strategy and oversee requirements (as per definition) implementation, collaborating across the organization to establish functional needs. Meanwhile, technical teams, including developers, architects, and data specialists, focus on addressing technical design (as per definition) as solution.

An Example Scenario

A simple but common scenario illustrates the alignment of business needs with a BI solution:

An organization sets a goal to increase conversion by 2 percent. To achieve this, management decides to either raise the number of sales or increase the value of each sale, requiring modifications to the sales process. Once implemented, management seeks to evaluate the most successful of these strategies by tracking the daily number and amount of sales. The data team is tasked with providing relevant sales data and generating associated reports or visualizations.

In the initial stages of a BI project, much of the knowledge required to design the solution exists implicitly or tacitly within the organization. The team will often need to engage in a maieutic process—a guided method of inquiry—to extract and formalize this information effectively.

Cold, Jumper, and Wool Analogy

Identifying and understanding key issues in complex environments can be challenging. Analysts and developers often rush into solution design without fully grasping the problem at hand. The cold, jumper, and wool analogy provides a framework for classifying needs and clarifying the distinction between problems and solutions. By changing wording, the business analyst is ensuring the vocabulary is unequivocal.

When functional stakeholders express their needs, they often focus on the solution, saying things like, "I need a report that does this ..." or "I need the data from this source." These statements may describe the desired outcome or technical design (as per definition), but they rarely address the requirement (as per definition). As a result, the data team may struggle to provide a solution that delivers real value.

The Analogy: Cold, Jumper, and Wool

Imagine a sheep farmer who knows how to knit wool and wants to start a business. A customer approaches with a request:

- "I want a jumper with white stripes and long sleeves." (functional design)
- They may also specify technical details: "I want it made out of wool." (technical design)

In this analogy:

- The wool and sheep represent the technical design (as per definition) (materials and resources).
- The jumper represents the functional (as per definition) (the product's features, such as size, color, and purpose).

However, neither the wool nor the jumper directly addresses the root need. The customer's real need is simple: "I'm cold." This is the business problem definition, which must be understood before any solution is designed.

Digging Deeper into the Problem

To craft the best solution, it is crucial to fully define the problem. Consider the following questions:

- Timing: Are you cold now, or are you preparing for next winter? (This determines urgency)
- Scope: Where are you cold? If it's only inside, perhaps closing the shutters and turning on the heater would suffice.
- Volume: How many people are cold? If it's just one, knitting needles may be enough. For a town, a factory might be more appropriate.
- Context: When and where are you cold? Are you Mike Horn going to North Pole? This might reveal additional opportunities, like using leftover wool to make socks.

Techniques for Problem Definition

Effective problem definition requires moving beyond predefined solutions and engaging stakeholders in meaningful conversations. Here are some useful techniques to guide the discussion:

- Ask about their goals: What does a good day look like? What about a bad day? What are they trying to achieve?
- Understand risks: What situations could lead to job losses?
- Explore incentives: What conditions would lead to a high bonus or recognition as "Employee of the Year" or "Forbes Best Leader"?
- Identify frustrations: What obstacles prevent them from achieving their goals?

These questions provide insight into stakeholders' KPIs, stresses, and responsibilities. Addressing their feelings and aspirations fosters collaboration and ensures the solution is aligned with their needs. Everyone wants to feel on top of their work while still having time for a coffee break.

Out-of-Scope Problems

It's equally important to acknowledge problems that are out of scope. Just because a need isn't addressed in the current project phase doesn't mean it ceases to exist. Out-of-scope needs may become part of the next project phase, require business or technical workarounds, or remain sources of frustration. Recognizing these needs ensures they are not forgotten and helps maintain realistic expectations.

Conclusion

The cold, jumper, and wool analogy emphasizes the importance of focusing on the business problem rather than jumping to solution design. By capturing the true problem definition and addressing both in-scope and out-of-scope needs, analysts and data teams can create solutions that provide maximum value to the business. This approach ensures alignment with business objectives, technical constraints, and stakeholder expectations.

Understanding How Data Is Processed Through: The Restaurant Analogy

The Kimball's restaurant analogy provides an effective way to illustrate how data is processed and requirements are gathered during a BI project. It simplifies complex concepts, making them more relatable to non-technical audiences. Additionally, it helps to communicate the workload, time, and effort involved in data processing, particularly for back-end tasks that are less visible to business stakeholders.

When stakeholders demand quick results, such as, "I need sales figures for the last six months, and I need them now," this analogy offers a humorous but effective response: "The data is still in the field—we haven't planted it yet." Such a response helps stakeholders quickly understand the feasibility of their requests and whether their timelines are realistic.

Food/Produce and Data

Like fruits and vegetables, data must go through a detailed process before it is ready for consumption. Just as a tomato needs to grow, be selected, cleaned, prepared, and seasoned before serving, data must also be historized, transformed, and processed with business rules and quality filters. It often needs to be combined with other data sources before it is ready for analysis and reporting.

Farming: Data Historization

A farmer's work—planting seeds, nurturing crops, and harvesting—requires effort, time, and patience. Similarly, data historization involves selecting, storing, and accumulating data chronologically to create a historical view of the organization. Although the operations may seem straightforward, the process is time-intensive and often goes unnoticed by stakeholders because it happens behind the scenes.

The Head Chef: Data Governance

In a restaurant, the Head Chef designs the menu, selects ingredients, and defines how they will be combined. In the BI context, data governance fulfills a similar role. It involves defining the organization's key metrics, dimensions, and rules for data usage. Governance establishes the "data menu" and determines who has access to which data, ensuring consistency and compliance.

The Nutritionist: Data Quality

The nutritionist ensures food is safe and nutritious by setting criteria and guidelines. In BI, data quality plays a similar role, ensuring that data is fit for consumption. Governance teams assess whether data meets the necessary standards for analysis, reporting, or legal compliance. High-quality data enables accurate forecasting and satisfies regulatory requirements.

The Cook: Data Modeling

The Cook transforms raw ingredients into a dish, just as the data modeler or engineer organizes, cleans, and integrates data. The goal is to prepare data in a way that analytics tools can consume it effectively. Business rules are applied, and the processed data becomes ready for visualization and reporting.

The Waiter: Visualization and Self-Service Analytics

The waiter's job in a restaurant is to prepare the table, recommend dishes, and serve meals. In BI, this stage corresponds to reporting and visualization. Dashboards can be created and monitored daily by specialists for executives, while self-service analytics allow users to build their own reports by accessing curated datasets. Like a buffet, this approach provides flexibility for users to tailor data to their needs.

Restaurant Analogy: Process and Timing

This analogy also helps explain how BI processes require preparation time at various stages, making it easier to estimate workloads and project timelines.

A Few Months Before: Data Historization

Building a robust data history begins well before the data is needed. If historization isn't done upfront, recreating historical data later can be extremely costly or even impossible. For example, regenerating five years of history from operational database logs or backups is an undesirable scenario. Thus, preparation is critical, akin to planting vegetables long before a chef needs them.

A Few Days Before: Data Transformation

A few days or months before the data is consumed, preparations begin. In a kitchen, this involves menu planning, purchasing ingredients, and prepping for service. Similarly, in BI, this phase includes transforming data, loading it into data marts or cubes, and defining standardized KPIs to ensure consistency across the organization.

A Few Minutes Before: Visualization Preparation

Just before the data is consumed, developers and analysts prepare reports, define visualization guidelines, and organize training for end-users. Much like setting the table and displaying specials in a restaurant, this stage ensures that stakeholders can quickly access and understand the information they need.

Restaurant Analogy: Granularity

Beyond processes and timing, the analogy also highlights the importance of granularity in requirements (as per Edward and al. [2000] model).

Strategic Granularity

Farmers don't need to know the exact plate or dish their carrots will end up on, but they do need to know the restaurant's overall strategy (e.g., vegan, organic, or focused on high-volume sales). Similarly, data historization requires knowledge of the data source's strategic importance, potential risks, and long-term value—not the specific tables or visualizations it will support.

Tactical Granularity

Kitchen staff can begin cooking without knowing exactly who will eat the meal. Likewise, developers can build the foundational elements of a data model (e.g., skeleton structures, key metrics, dimensions) without finalizing every visualization. However, care must be taken to avoid designing models solely for individual visualizations, as this can lead to duplication and inefficiencies in later stages.

Operational Granularity

At the operational level, the focus shifts to specifics, such as individual orders, customer allergies, or special requests. In BI, this corresponds to the final stages of data delivery, where the requirements align with user expectations. Techniques like prototyping or self-service analytics help clarify user needs and ensure that the solution is both functional and adaptable.

Conclusion

The restaurant analogy simplifies complex BI processes, making it easier for stakeholders to understand requirements, timing, and granularity. By using relatable examples, this analogy helps foster better communication, align expectations, and ensure successful project outcomes. Whether preparing a gourmet meal or delivering actionable insights, the key to success lies in careful planning and execution.

Business Analysis Process

The Business Requirements Process

The business requirements process encompasses eight key subprocesses, each comprising specific activities (Figure 2.5):

1. Elicitation and Capture
2. Modeling
3. Specification
4. Prioritization
5. Dependencies Management
6. Impact Evaluation
7. Negotiation
8. Quality Management

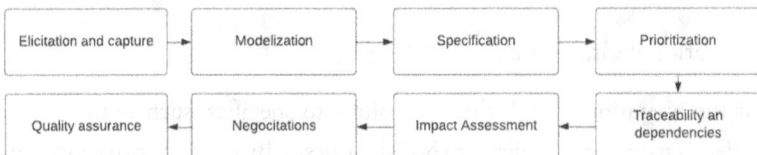

Figure 2.5 Overview of the requirement management process

Elicitation and Capture

This initial phase focuses on gathering comprehensive needs from all stakeholders and sources. The analyst conducts interviews and workshops to accurately document these requirements, ensuring a thorough understanding of stakeholder expectations.

Modeling

In the modeling phase, the collected requirements are organized into a coherent structure. Techniques such as goal trees or concept models are employed to visualize and articulate these needs, facilitating clearer communication among team members.

Specification

During specification, the analyst refines the requirements to be precise, actionable, and free from ambiguities. This step ensures that the documented needs are implementable and align with the project's objectives.

Prioritization

This phase involves ranking the requirements based on their importance and urgency. It helps in resolving conflicts and determining which needs will be addressed within the project's constraints, ensuring that critical requirements receive priority.

Dependencies Management

Here, the interrelationships between requirements are identified and managed. Understanding these dependencies is crucial to prevent conflicts and ensure a smooth implementation process.

Impact Evaluation

This phase assesses how each requirement aligns with the project's goals, budget, and timelines. The objective is to determine the feasibility and value of each requirement by evaluating its potential business impact, technical complexity, and resource demand. This step helps ensure that the most critical and high-value requirements are prioritized while identifying dependencies and constraints that might affect implementation. A thorough impact evaluation helps prevent scope creep and ensures the project remains aligned with strategic objectives.

Negotiation

Once the impact of each requirement is assessed, stakeholders engage in negotiation to finalize the project's scope. This involves discussions between business teams, technical teams, and project sponsors to balance needs with available resources. Some requirements may be deferred, modified, or removed based on feasibility, cost-benefit analysis, or alignment with business priorities. Effective negotiation ensures that all parties agree on realistic expectations, trade-offs, and deliverables, reducing friction later in the project life cycle.

Quality Management

Quality management involves defining clear criteria to ensure that the developed solution meets stakeholder expectations. Establishing these standards early in the process guides developers and sets benchmarks for evaluating the final product's success.

Implementation Considerations

While it's uncommon for all these steps to be fully implemented in practice, understanding each phase highlights the risks of omission. This knowledge enables teams to make informed decisions tailored to their project's context.

Notably, separating the elicitation phase from negotiation allows stakeholders to express all their needs without immediate constraints. This approach can uncover existing solutions within the organization, provide quick wins, and offer a comprehensive view of current challenges and future opportunities. It provides a big picture view and a sustainable solution.

Elicitation and Capture

The elicitation and capture phase marks the beginning of the requirements process. This step is often referred to as the "trawling phase," drawing inspiration from the fishing practice of casting a wide net to collect everything underwater—coral, fish, and mammals alike. At this stage, all stakeholders and potential requirements are listed without regard to feasibility, budget, or priority. It's a creative and exploratory phase, where stakeholders can freely express their needs and ideas, no matter how ambitious or exaggerated they may seem.

Why Is This Step Important?

Listening to all stakeholders, even when their requirements fall outside the immediate scope of the initiative, is essential. This approach:

- Offers insights into the organization's strategic goals that the product must support now or later
- Highlights potential frustrations and challenges the project team may face
- Provides a clearer picture of subsequent project phases, aiding long-term planning

The elicitation process is divided into five key activities:

1. Understanding the application domain
2. Identifying sources of needs
3. Analyzing stakeholders
4. Selecting techniques and tools
5. Eliciting requirements from stakeholders and other sources

Understanding the Business Domain

This step involves gaining a deep understanding of the subject matter, including the business objectives, supporting processes, organizational policies, and operational requirements. It's not about identifying specific visualizations or reports; rather, it's about understanding the environment in which the solution will operate and how it aligns with business goals.

Identifying Sources of Requirements

The next step is to list all possible sources of requirements. These can include:

- People: Users, subject matter experts, and stakeholders, technical team
- Systems: Existing or legacy systems
- Documentation: Legal documents, manuals, and reports, existing documentation

During the trawling phase, selecting sources for detailed analysis is unnecessary. Instead, the goal is to create a comprehensive list that can be referenced and refined later as the process progresses.

Stakeholder Analysis

Stakeholders are individuals or groups, internal or external, who have an interest in or are impacted by the project. Their influence can be positive or negative, and their roles must be clearly identified during the trawling phase.

Examples of potential stakeholders include:

- Users and their representatives
- Current process managers
- Standards and security managers
- Partners and suppliers
- Legal teams and infrastructure managers
- People downstream of the process who will be impacted
- Technical team

Even stakeholders who may not seem directly involved can play a critical role by providing insights, resolving challenges, or influencing decisions.

Selecting Techniques and Tools

The success of requirements gathering depends on choosing the right methods and tools. Contextual factors, such as cultural differences, stakeholder expertise, and organizational dynamics, play a significant role in this decision. The business analyst may choose to conduct a code review with a technical stakeholder, but this approach would not be suitable for a functional stakeholder. Similarly, the analyst might use a goal tree approach when meeting with a top manager who can only allocate 30 minutes, while preferring a process design discussion with the person responsible for daily operations.

Some common techniques include:

- Interviews: Ideal for one-on-one discussions with time-constrained stakeholders
- Workshops: Effective for gathering input from multiple stakeholders simultaneously and fostering collaboration

Your organization may have guidelines or frameworks to assist in selecting the most suitable approaches. Analysts trained in requirements gathering can adapt these techniques or combine them to meet the needs of diverse stakeholders. Most projects benefit from a mix of group and individual approaches to ensure inclusivity and completeness. A comprehensive list of techniques is available in Chapter 3, Business Analysis Techniques section.

Eliciting Requirements from Stakeholders and Other Sources

Once the business domain is understood, stakeholders are identified, and sources are listed, the focus shifts to formulating requirements. This step is iterative and may involve repeating or combining techniques to achieve clarity and alignment.

Elicitation often requires multiple phases:

- Functional needs: These are the business needs or user require-ments, focusing on defining business problems or supporting processes.
- Technical designs: (often call technical requirement) These detail the technical components and design specifications needed to de-liver the functional requirements. Abstract models of the system may be created at this stage to:
  1. Help developers understand what needs to be built.
  2. Ensure the solution design aligns with the functional require-ments (Figure 2.6).

Modelization

Following the elicitation and capture phase, the modelization process be-gins. A model serves as a simplified representation of reality, created with a specific objective in mind. This objective-driven approach is crucial to ensure the model effectively supports the project's goals.

Models formalize requirements at a conceptual level. There may be one or multiple models, depending on the complexity of the project. These models detail what needs to be done, including which systems and visualizations must be created or modified. The process of modelization not only highlights potential issues but also supports problem-solving and enables analysts or developers to design the most efficient solution possible.

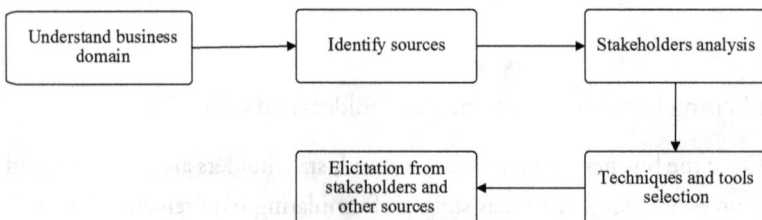

Figure 2.6 Overview of the elicitation process

Distinction Between Elicitation and Modelization

The boundary between elicitation and capture and modelization and specification can sometimes appear unclear. However, their focus differs:

- Elicitation and capture concentrate on understanding the problem that needs to be addressed.
- Modelization and specification aim to develop and define the solution.

The primary goal of modelization is to adopt a uniform language to reduce ambiguities and ensure a successful implementation.

Approaches to Modelization

The choice of modeling technique depends on the objective of the model. Various graphical representations can be employed to illustrate processes, data models, or user interfaces. While the list of techniques is extensive, some of the most commonly used in BI include:

- Process models for mapping workflows and operational sequences
- Data models for organizing and structuring data
- User interface mock-ups for visualizing how users will interact with the solution

Specification Phase

Once the appropriate modeling techniques are selected, the next step is to model the system. Regardless of the approach chosen, the specification phase should address three key criteria: the language used, complexity management, and continuity management. These criteria ensure that the models are clear, manageable, and aligned with project objectives.

Language

The language used in specifications is crucial for ensuring clarity and effective communication. This language may be:

- Formal: Enables automation of development processes by being highly precise
- Semiformal: Facilitates communication between stakeholders and developers while maintaining enough structure to guide implementation

Regardless of the type, the chosen language must:

- Minimize ambiguities to avoid misinterpretation.
- Ensure the specifications are reproducible.
- Allow for proper testing of the final solution.

For further details on linguistic considerations, refer to Chapter 3, Syntax and Grammar Analysis section.

Complexity Management

A system may be either complicated or complex:

- Complicated systems involve numerous interacting components. For example: A data warehouse needs to integrate 150 internal tables from various operational systems, each with well-documented data structures. The relationships between the tables are known, the formats are standardized, and the integration rules are clearly specified. The work requires significant technical expertise and careful coordination, but once the design is validated, execution is predictable.
  Here, the system is complicated because it has many parts, but they are mostly well understood and can be fully specified upfront.
- Complex systems involve diverse, dynamic, and unpredictable interactions. For example: a BI solution needs to consolidate

data from internal customer relationship management (CRM) systems, partner APIs (application programming interfaces), customer e-mails, unstructured complaint logs, external social media feeds, and government open data. The data arrives in multiple formats (structured, semistructured, unstructured), at different frequencies, and with varying data quality. The way these data sources interact may change over time as business priorities or data providers evolve.

In short, "complicated" refers to systems with many known parts, predictable behavior, expertise required but are manageable, while "complex" describes systems with unpredictable interactions, changing conditions, and emergent behavior, thus requiring adaptability.

Managing complexity effectively involves addressing two types:

1. Representation Complexity: This arises when systems are heterogeneous or when the objective of the model is unclear. Overloading models with excessive details often results in unreadable and impractical representations.
2. Development Complexity: This relates to changes in the model and managing different versions effectively.

The simplest way to manage complexity is by grouping specifications to reduce the number of components. Striking the right balance between generalization and detail ensures the model remains readable while preserving its meaning. Abstraction levels must facilitate communication without sacrificing the essence of the requirements.

Continuity Management

Continuity management ensures alignment and coherence between:

- Business objectives
- Needs analysis
- Solution design
- Implementation

Maintaining traceability between these stages minimizes rework and simplifies the management of changes. Continuity management reduces workloads and ensures a streamlined process.

To achieve this:

- Each step of the requirements process must be modeled independently but linked to the previous and subsequent stages.
- Changes in implementation should only require modifications to specific downstream components, avoiding the need to revisit the entire project scope.

Steps in the Continuity Model

The continuity model involves four interconnected layers:

1. Business Objectives: These represent the organization's overarching goals.
2. Needs Analysis: Functional needs are formalized and interpreted. It's the definition of the problem to be solved.
3. Design: The solution model is developed to address the functional requirements, including all solution functionalities. It's the definition of the solution.
4. Implementation: The physical implementation (e.g., code, scripts) is created based on the design. It's the solution.

By maintaining connections between these layers, analysts can quickly identify impacted components and limit the scope of changes.

Practical Applications of Continuity Management

Though theoretical at first glance, the continuity model provides tangible benefits when applied:

- Impact Analysis: Changes can be isolated to specific components or layers.

- Consistency: Reusable components reduce redundancy and ensure alignment across the solution.
- Efficiency: Duplicate code, tables, or reports are quickly identified and eliminated.

Example: Consider a company transitioning from local retail shops to online sales. By clearly documenting the relationships between business objectives, functional requirements, design, and implementation, integrating online sales data into the existing data mart becomes straightforward. The continuity model helps identify this as a new business event tied to a different data source, minimizing rework and ensuring consistent development.

Tools for Implementing the Continuity Model

To link different layers of the continuity model effectively, several tools and models can be employed:

- Goals Trees: For defining business objectives and functional needs
- Business Process Models: To represent workflows, such as online sales processes
- Data Process Models: To map data flows, including operational systems supporting sales. It's the context the solution will be integrated to.
- Extract, Transform, Load (ETL) and Data Models: To illustrate how data from various sources (e.g., X and Y) is loaded into target tables (e.g., "SALES").

Explicit modeling of each layer makes it easier to assess the impact of changes. For instance, adjustments in the sales process can be traced through to data sources, ETL processes, and reporting systems, ensuring alignment and minimizing disruptions (Figure 2.7).

Prioritization: A Critical Phase in Requirement Management

The prioritization phase is vital in determining which requirements will fall within the project's scope and which will not. During this stage,

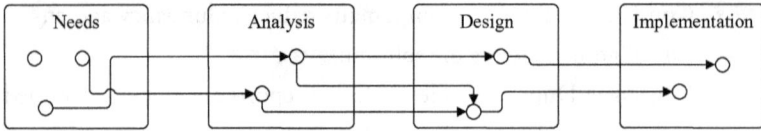

Figure 2.7 Steps of the continuity model

the team balances the desires of business stakeholders with project constraints, such as time, budget, and nonfunctional requirements. Effective prioritization maximizes stakeholder satisfaction while minimizing the overall workload. This phase also helps manage requirement conflicts and maintain the motivation of both functional and technical stakeholders.

Prioritization is often viewed as the most political activity in the requirement management process. It involves selecting the "right" requirements from among many, ensuring alignment with business goals, user preferences, and technical constraints while maximizing product value—a significant and complex undertaking.

Various techniques are available for prioritization, ranging from quantitative methods to qualitative approaches such as negotiation. However, asking stakeholders directly, "What's most important from your perspective?" is insufficient. Stakeholders, influenced by personal agendas, differing personalities, and changing priorities, may favor short-term benefits over long-term strategic goals. Skipping this phase is often a strategic mistake, as poor prioritization can lead to significant project risks.

Prioritization Criteria

The first step in prioritization is to establish evaluation criteria. Common criteria include:

- Significance: This varies based on stakeholders' perspectives. Certain tasks may hold higher importance for business users, final users, or the development team.
- Penalties: Legal or regulatory requirements may impose penalties for noncompliance. In some cases, the organization may opt to delay compliance if penalties are low and the need is not urgent.

- Cost: This includes both the cost of development and maintenance and the potential business cost if the feature is not implemented. Cost analysis often involves cost-opportunity comparisons. Costs can be estimated in financial terms (e.g., dollars) or time (e.g., person-days). It's usually the most scarce resource.
- Time: Refers to both the time needed for development and the time required to train users if the solution is not intuitive. The team may identify tasks that can run in parallel to save time.
- Risk: Risks may include financial losses, reduced performance, harm to the organization's reputation, or delays in planning and deadlines. Critical risks often require integration into formal project management processes, such as a risk register.
- Volatility: In fast-changing environments, initial requirements may lose relevance due to shifts in market conditions, strategy, or new legal measures.
- Dependencies: Certain tasks depend on the completion of others. Nonfunctional needs, such as infrastructure and security, are typically prioritized alongside their associated functional requirements.

Once criteria are established, the analyst selects a prioritization technique appropriate to the project's context.

Prioritization Techniques

Hierarchical Analysis

This method involves listing tasks in order of priority. While simple to implement, it becomes challenging to manage large sets of requirements effectively and doesn't give much information in terms of urgency.

Cumulative Voting

Known as the "100-dollar bill test," participants are given a limited amount of currency (e.g., points, dollars) to distribute among requirements. Rules can be adjusted to ensure fairness and prevent skewed results, such as limiting how much can be allocated to a single requirement or requiring participants to distribute their votes across multiple items. This technique works well with clear rules and sufficient stakeholder engagement but is best suited for single iterations to avoid influencing subsequent rounds.

Grouping Method

A common approach that organizes requirements into categories, such as:

- Must-have
- Should-have
- Could-have
- Won't-have

The MoSCoW method is a widely recognized version of this approach. However, stakeholders often label too many requirements as "must-have," reducing the effectiveness of this technique. To address this, a cap on the number of high-priority items may be imposed.

Ranking Method

This technique involves listing requirements in order of importance. It is effective when all requirements have similar levels of granularity but fails to measure the relative importance of one requirement over another. Sorting methods, such as bubble or dichotomous sorts, can assist in managing rankings.

Top 10 Method

Each stakeholder selects their top 10 requirements, and those appearing most frequently are prioritized. While simple and quick, this method may fail to resolve conflicts between stakeholders or address the needs of all parties equitably. It is best suited for low-stakes decisions or initial project phases.

Selecting and Refining Prioritization Methods

Choosing the Right Method

Not all prioritization methods are equally easy to implement, and the choice of method often depends on balancing effort with output quality. The analyst and project manager must consider the level of granularity required for prioritization. For instance:

- Is it sufficient to group requirements into categories?
- Will prioritization need to account for budgetary constraints?

The number of requirements is also a critical factor. For example, if there are only ten requirements, a "Top 10" method would not provide meaningful differentiation.

Combining Techniques

With proper planning, combining multiple techniques can reduce costs and improve efficiency. This approach is similar to triage in hospital emergency services during crises, where patients are prioritized based on the potential impact of care.

In a prioritization context:

1. Initial Sorting: Divide requirements into broad categories, such as:
   - Critical (Must-Have): Essential components like platforms, databases, and security features (in scope)
   - Optional (Nice-to-Have): Nonessential elements like aesthetic features (might be out of scope)
   - Refinable: Key functionalities requiring further prioritization to determine inclusion in scope
2. Fine-Tuning: Apply detailed prioritization techniques to the critical and refinable group only, ensuring efficient use of time and resources.

Adding Creativity to the Process

Introducing creativity can make the prioritization process more engaging and improve stakeholder participation. For example:

- Cumulative Voting: Replace "currency" with sticker dots, monopoly money, or candies.
- Hierarchical Analysis: Use Post-its or magnets to create an interactive experience.

While tools like Jira or Excel can facilitate prioritization, even simple methods can benefit from creative touches to keep stakeholders engaged.

Stakeholder Involvement

Prioritization becomes increasingly complex as more stakeholders are involved, each bringing unique opinions, needs, and constraints. To manage this complexity, three perspectives must be considered:

- Functional Needs: Typically identified by business stakeholders, representing the "why" behind the solution. Without addressing functional needs, there is a risk of building solutions that are not used.
- Technical Needs: These emerge from project teams and technical stakeholders, addressing constraints, sustainability, and best practices.
- Financial Needs: Defined by sponsors or project managers, these establish the budgetary framework for development.

Balancing these perspectives ensures a fair process and prevents any single stakeholder from dominating. Weighted approaches can reflect the varying importance of stakeholders while ensuring inclusivity to avoid demotivation or opposition.

Managing Granularity

Requirements are rarely expressed at the same level of granularity, making direct comparisons challenging. Grouping requirements into similar levels of detail can help:

- In Agile practices, tools like Jira group items into epics, stories, and tasks for easier comparison.
- Comparing epics with other epics and tasks with other tasks ensures meaningful prioritization.

Avoiding comparisons across different levels of granularity simplifies decision making and enhances accuracy.

Reprioritization as an Iterative Process

Prioritization is not a one-time activity. Stakeholder priorities, project scope, and solution designs can evolve, necessitating adjustments. By incorporating a continuity model, changes can be isolated to directly impacted and downstream components, minimizing disruption. Moreover, requiring justifications for changes prevents unnecessary reprioritization.

Prioritizing Nonfunctional Requirements

Nonfunctional requirements must also be prioritized. These can be grouped into:

1. Objectives: High-level goals the system aims to achieve
2. Decisions: Qualitative descriptions of system behavior
3. Design Constraints: Quantitative objectives derived from decisions

Nonfunctional needs often differentiate between implementation options. For example, if two solutions meet functional needs, nonfunctional requirements like performance, security, or scalability may guide the decision.

Conclusion

Selecting the right prioritization method involves balancing simplicity, stakeholder engagement, and the granularity of requirements. Combining techniques, fostering creativity, and involving stakeholders ensure a robust and inclusive process. By managing requirements at the appropriate level of granularity and considering nonfunctional needs, the process becomes more adaptable and aligned with project goals.

Reprioritization should be embraced as an iterative process, supported by continuity models to minimize disruption and maximize efficiency. Thoughtful prioritization ultimately drives project success and delivers value to all stakeholders.

Traceability and Dependency Management

Managing traceability and dependencies is a critical aspect of requirement management. It ensures the alignment of project components with objectives, reduces the risk of rework, and enhances the quality, integrity, and manageability of the system. Poorly managed dependencies can lead to project delays, increased costs, and misunderstandings. Traceability ensures that all components are accounted for and their relationships understood, while dependency management addresses the interconnections and impacts between requirements.

Traceability

Traceability provides a clear link between requirements and their origins, ensuring every component supports project objectives. It serves multiple purposes, including impact analysis, requirement validation, and ensuring alignment across project phases.

- Pre-traceability: This links business domains with requirements. For example, if a business objective is to improve customer satisfaction, the associated need might be to analyze customer dissatisfaction data.
- Post-traceability: This assesses the impact of implementing or modifying requirements and forms the basis for testing.

Traceability can occur in multiple forms:

- Vertical Traceability: This links requirements at different abstraction levels, such as a high-level objective ("increase sales by 20%") to a more granular requirement ("achieve a 20% increase in sales through new client acquisition"). This ensures consistency and prevents redundancy.
- Horizontal Traceability: This connects requirements of the same granularity that are interdependent. For example, a sales tracking table could simultaneously address "track salesforce performance" and "identify low-margin products."

Dependencies

Dependencies outline the relationships between requirements and their mutual influences. They can be categorized into structural, constraint, and cost/value dependencies (Figure 2.8).

Structural Dependencies

There are multiple types of dependencies such as:

- Structural dependencies highlight hierarchical relationships or changes in requirements.
- Hierarchical Dependencies: Higher-level requirements (e.g., "create a sales report") may include or clarify lower-level requirements (e.g., "generate monthly regional sales reports"). Understanding these dependencies ensures that all levels of requirements align with project objectives and facilitates grouping similar needs.
- Change Dependencies: Managing changes in requirements, such as shifting from "weekly data refresh" to "daily data refresh," ensures impacts are understood and communicated. This minimizes complexity and rework.
- Similarity Dependencies: Some requirements share common elements and can be grouped. For example, "reports available offline" is similar to "reports accessible during client meetings." Identifying such similarities streamlines requirement management.

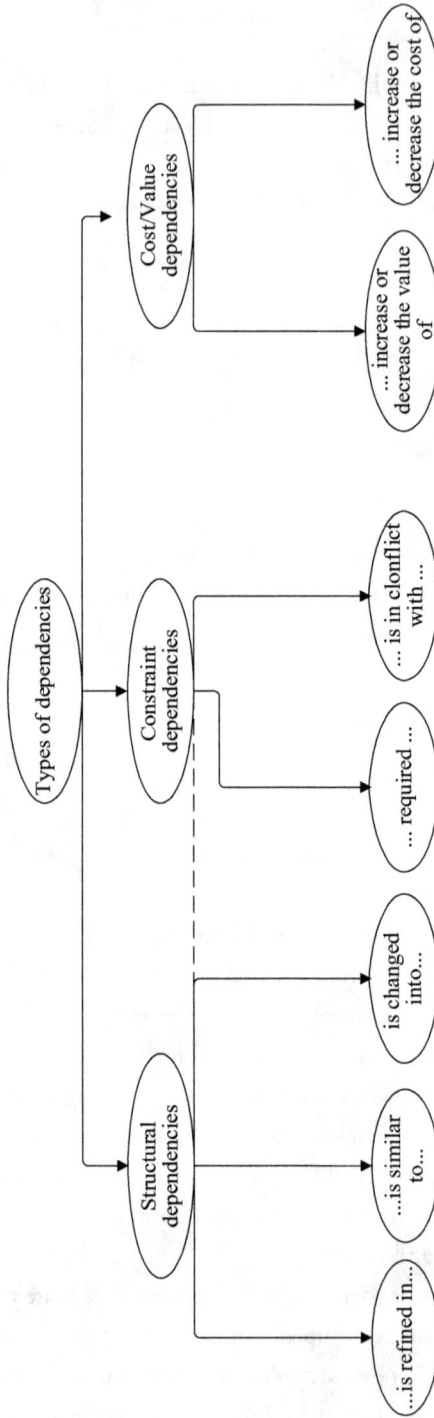

Figure 2.8 Dependencies model

Constraint Dependencies

Constraint dependencies arise when the completion of one requirement depends on another.

- Precedence Dependencies: For instance, a database cannot exist without a server. These dependencies determine implementation order and ensure prerequisites are met.
- Conflicting Dependencies: Some requirements may conflict, such as performance requirements versus data volume needs. For example, "dashboard load time under 2 seconds" may conflict with "display 10 years of historical data." Balancing these conflicts requires careful negotiation and prioritization. Often the solution will be a compromise and partially meets those requirements.

Cost and Value Dependencies

Certain requirements influence the cost or perceived value of others:

- Cost Dependencies: For instance, adding a security layer increases the cost of making a solution mobile-accessible.
- Value Dependencies: A requirement like "export reports in PDF format" enhances the perceived value of "generate monthly sales reports."

The objective is to identify these dependencies to optimize prioritization, ensuring the best trade-offs between cost, value, and impact.

Conclusion

Effective traceability and dependency management are vital for aligning requirements with project goals, managing changes, and optimizing resources. By maintaining clear connections between requirements and addressing their interdependencies, teams can reduce complexity, minimize rework, and deliver higher-quality solutions.

This structured approach ensures the project remains agile and adaptable, balancing functional, technical, and business considerations while maximizing stakeholder satisfaction.

Impact Assessment

Evaluating the impact of changes within a project is critical for maintaining quality and minimizing risks. Various methods can be used, with some being more precise than others. The effectiveness of an impact assessment depends on the type of information required and the chosen technique. The goal is to ensure the assessment is not overly costly while still producing actionable and reliable results.

Human Bias

Human bias significantly influences impact assessment, as highlighted by Lindvall and Sandahl (1998) in their study published in the *Journal of Systems and Software*. The research demonstrates that senior developers tend to underestimate the effort required to implement changes by an average factor of three, meaning actual costs are often three times higher than initial estimates.

Developers often aim to satisfy stakeholders and management or project competence, leading to optimistic estimates. Bias can also stem from a lack of expertise, resulting in overly conservative or overly optimistic projections. Strategies to mitigate bias include:

- Collaborative Decision Making: Involving multiple individuals to assess impacts and averaging their estimates or adopting the most conservative estimate. Differences in estimates can spark discussions to refine understanding.
- Structured Review: Encouraging team discussions to ensure shared knowledge about complexity or potential risks.

Collaborative approaches enhance the accuracy of impact analysis and offer opportunities for learning. For instance, tracking estimates against actual outcomes fosters continuous improvement. To make the process engaging, incentives for the most accurate estimate can be introduced.

Impact analysis serves as a valuable tool for managing changes while minimizing quality degradation. It helps identify costs, consequences, and side effects, enabling cost/benefit evaluations.

Vocabulary

Understanding terminology is essential for effective impact assessment:

- SLOs (Software Life Cycle Objects): These are IT components generated during the project, such as tables, reports, cubes, and connections, interconnected through dependencies.
- SIS (Starting Impact Set): The set of SLOs directly affected by a proposed change
- EIS (Estimated Impact Set): A broader set of SLOs assessed as being directly or indirectly impacted by the change
- AIS (Actual Impact Set): The final set of SLOs impacted by the change after implementation

Reasons for Changes

Change is an inherent part of projects and can arise from several factors:

1. External Environment: Shifts in market conditions, regulatory updates, or technological advancements (e.g., data mining or AI upgrades)
2. Process Discoveries: As the team works through existing processes, inefficiencies or errors may be identified, necessitating changes to optimize workflows.
3. Evolving Stakeholder Needs: Stakeholders often refine their needs as they gain a deeper understanding of the project, or due to changes in personnel or organizational priorities.

Change, in itself, is not inherently negative. For example, when a project progresses smoothly, stakeholders may become more engaged, leading to scope expansion or the introduction of new requirements. Challenges arise only when changes are poorly managed.

Proposed Framework

A commonly accepted change management framework consists of five steps:

1. Change Plan: Establishing awareness and initiating the process for addressing the change
2. Point of Comparison: Creating a copy of the original requirement to serve as a baseline for evaluation
3. Unique Channel: Centralizing all changes through a single channel for tracking and processing
4. Control Management System: Evaluating costs, risks (such as introducing bugs), functionality impacts, and user implications. A change management committee often performs this step.
5. Hierarchy Management: Implementing changes methodically, following a structured continuity model to ensure alignment with project objectives (Figure 2.9)

In addition, Kotonya and Sommerville (1998) propose a detailed change management process, comprising three stages:

1. Analyzing the Problem and Specifying the Change: Identifying the root cause of the change and defining it as a requirement
2. Cost Analysis: Evaluating the validity, benefits, and costs of the change, as well as its broader implications. This includes assessing SIS and EIS components and evaluating the acceptability of the change.
3. Change Implementation: Implementing the change and integrating it within the existing system

These frameworks provide comprehensive guidelines for managing changes effectively, minimizing disruptions, and maintaining project continuity (Figure 2.10).

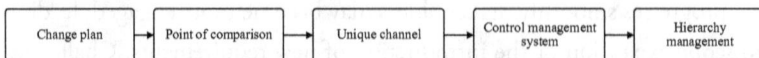

| Change plan | → | Point of comparison | → | Unique channel | → | Control management system | → | Hierarchy management |

Figure 2.9 Change management framework

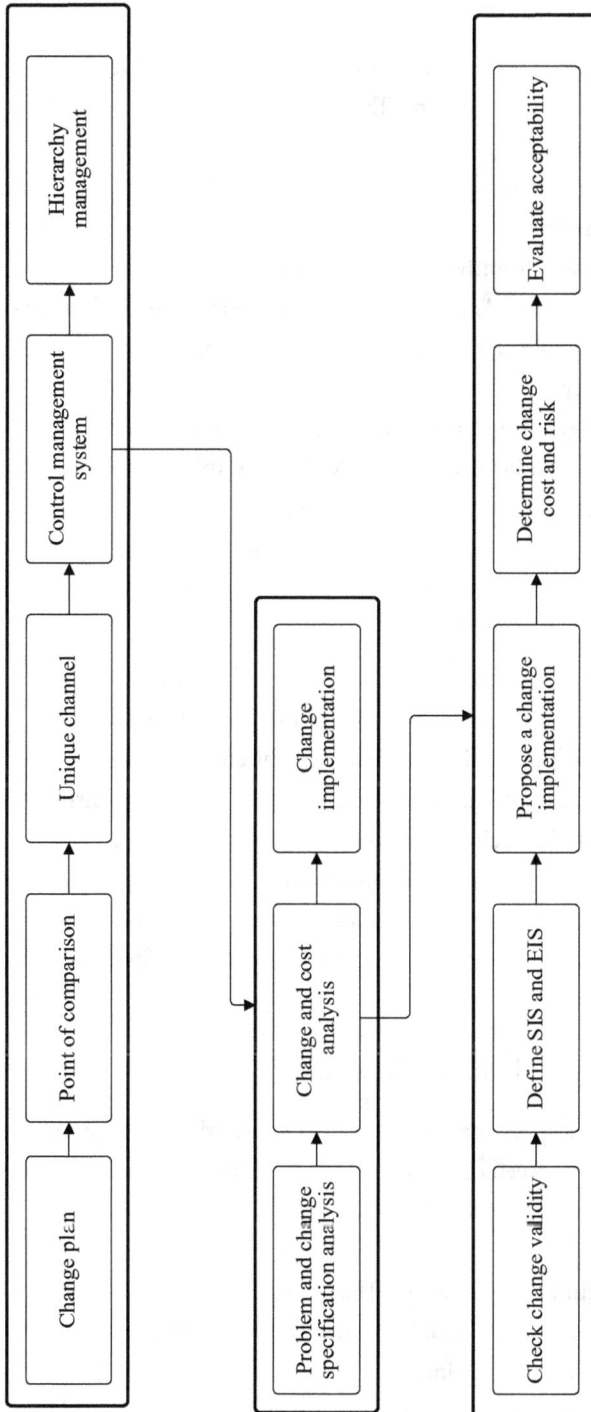

Figure 2.10 Detailed change management framework

Manual Approaches

Manual approaches are straightforward and cost-effective but require substantial effort from the team. They include:

1. Documentation Analysis: Reviewing existing documentation to assess the impact of changes. The quality and relevance of documentation significantly influence the outcome.
2. Code Review: Analyzing scripts or code for a detailed understanding of the system. This is time-consuming but ensures high accuracy.
3. Interviews: Engaging with developers, particularly the script's original author, for insights. While efficient, this method is constrained by the availability of key personnel.

Automated Approaches

Automation is feasible if dependencies and the continuity model are well documented. Automated approaches can accurately assess SIS and EIS components but require significant initial effort for dependency definition. In practice, partial automation is often the most realistic and effective solution, balancing precision with practicality.

By leveraging a traceability matrix, teams can achieve detailed analyses without the upfront costs of full automation. This hybrid approach optimizes impact assessment while remaining resource-efficient.

Costs Associated with Impact Analysis

The cost of impact analysis depends significantly on the acceptable margin of error between optimistic and conservative estimates, which directly ties to the project's risk tolerance.

- Optimistic Estimation: This is usually based on the SIS, which includes only the objects directly affected by the change.
- Conservative Estimation: This incorporates the EIS, which accounts for both direct and indirect impacts.

If the estimation is overly conservative, the size of the SIS and EIS (direct and indirect objects) will significantly exceed the AIS, thereby leading to inefficiencies in cost management.

Minimizing Analysis Costs

Reducing the costs of impact analysis requires balancing the risks associated with development, potential bugs, and data quality issues. A foundational technique for this is creating a traceability and dependencies matrix, also known as an impact matrix (Figure 2.11).

Traceability and Dependencies Matrix

This matrix functions as a pivot table, identifying which source objects (SIS) affect which target objects (EIS). It can be built manually or through automated script analysis (Figure 2.12).

- Columns: Represent targets (EIS)
- Rows: Represent sources (SIS)

Experts should review the initial matrix to refine and confirm the list of potential impacts. Without this critical review, the estimates may become excessively conservative, with all system objects appearing as potentially impacted, especially when considering ripple effects.

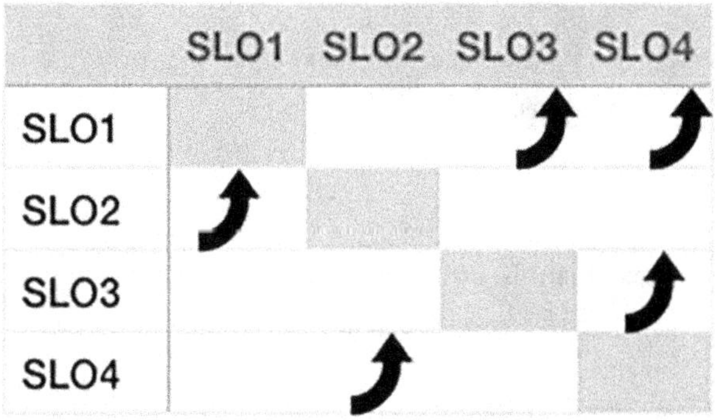

Figure 2.11 Traceability and dependencies matrix

		EIS	
		Change	Without Change
AIS	Change	%$^{(1)}$	%$^{(2)}$
	Without change	%$^{(3)}$	%$^{(4)}$

Figure 2.12 Number of EIS objects versus the number of AIS objects matrix

Continuous Improvement Approach

By comparing the EIS and AIS, teams can refine the traceability matrix over time, leading to more accurate estimates and lower analysis costs for future changes.

Managing Ripple Effect Risks

The ripple effect occurs when indirect impacts cascade beyond the immediate changes. These are often referred to as "riddles"—objects indirectly affected at levels beyond the immediate impact.

- Example: Changing the definition of "Customer" affects the "Customer" dimension, which cascades to related fact tables and additional dimensions.

Mitigation

To minimize ripple effects:

1. Identify the targets of the change.
2. Iteratively review the traceability matrix, using outputs as inputs for subsequent analysis.

Quantifying Impact

Effective impact analysis not only identifies affected objects but also quantifies the effort and cost involved. Metrics include:

- Indirect Impact Risks: Ratio of SIS objects to EIS objects. A ratio close to 1 indicates manageable risks.

- Magnitude of Change: Ratio of EIS objects to total system components. A lower ratio suggests minimal disruption.

Accuracy of Estimates: Ratio of EIS to AIS objects. Ideally, this should be close to 1, signifying accurate predictions.
Inclusion Indicator: Verifies whether all AIS objects are accounted for in the EIS. A value of 1 indicates a complete analysis.

Matrix for Impact Estimation

A comparison matrix can evaluate the alignment between EIS and AIS objects, categorizing predictions into accurate forecasts, unidentified impacts (risks), or overly conservative estimates.

	EIS: Change	EIS: No Change
AIS: Change	(1) Good prediction (%)	(2) Missed impacts (%)
AIS: No Change	(3) Overconservatism (%)	(4) Accurate exclusions (%)

The goal is to maximize percentages (1) and (4) while minimizing (2) and (3).

Reducing Impact Costs

Minimizing impact costs extends beyond analysis to include development techniques that compartmentalize systems. Examples include:

1. Layered Architecture: Splitting data warehouses into stages (staging, integration, presentation) reduces the ripple effect of changes.
2. Vocabulary Glossaries: Standardizing KPIs prevents redundant development efforts.

The Art of Negotiation: Defining Project Scope

The negotiation phase is a critical component of the requirement management process, especially in BI projects. This stage often involves extensive discussions and arguments, facilitated by conflict resolution techniques derived from various domains such as social sciences, game theory, psychology, and decision-making theory. While this chapter provides a high-level overview, detailed negotiation techniques remain beyond the scope of this book. Broadly, the negotiation process consists of three stages: prenegotiation, negotiation, and postnegotiation.

Advantages of Negotiation

The negotiation phase offers several key benefits:

1. Understanding Project Constraints
   Stakeholders exchange views on technical, budgetary, and functional constraints, fostering mutual understanding and helping to identify the best compromise between these constraints.
2. Facilitating Change Management
   Scope or technical solution changes are debated and better understood, enabling stakeholders to accept decisions more readily.
3. Encouraging Learning
   The team gains insights into functional and technical aspects. Junior team members can ask questions, fostering knowledge transfer within the team and with external stakeholders.
4. Uncovering Tacit Knowledge
   Often, stakeholders consider certain aspects self-evident and may not articulate them. Negotiations help surface this implicit knowledge.
5. Managing Complexity
   By addressing and debating complex issues collaboratively, the negotiation process often simplifies them and ensures alignment among stakeholders.
6. Managing Uncertainty
   Technical constraints and feasibility are clarified for nontechnical stakeholders, improving their understanding of project challenges and feasibility.
7. Improving Solutions
   Discussions may lead to optimal solutions that reflect compromises and incorporate diverse perspectives.

Prenegotiation Phase

The prenegotiation phase focuses on framing the problem, identifying stakeholders, and analyzing their objectives.

1. Defining the Problem
   Clear problem definition sets the stage for focused discussions. At the beginning of a project, negotiations are high-level but become more detailed as the project progresses. Keeping discussions at the appropriate level of detail prevents getting sidetracked.
2. Identifying Stakeholders
   Ensuring the right stakeholders are present is critical for durable decisions. Missing stakeholders might invalidate agreements, leading to later opposition and redundant negotiations.
3. Analyzing Objectives
   Eliciting and understanding each stakeholder's objectives enables the identification of obstacles and conflicting interests. These objectives, often tied to the system's desired outcomes, vary in granularity and require reformulation and organization for meaningful comparisons.

Negotiation Phase

This phase involves structured discussions to explore ideas and develop alternative solutions, typically based on compromises that balance stakeholder interests.

1. Announcing Objectives
   Clearly communicating the negotiation's objectives allows stakeholders to prepare and, if necessary, formulate strategies.
2. Conflict Resolution Strategies
   Borrowing from community psychology, Thomas and Killman identified five conflict resolution strategies:
   ○ Competing: One stakeholder prioritizes their needs at the expense of others.

- ○ Collaborating: Stakeholders work together to achieve a mutually beneficial "win-win" solution.
- ○ Compromising: Stakeholders agree on partial fulfillment of their requirements when full satisfaction isn't possible.
- ○ Avoiding: Stakeholders disengage, often through absenteeism or nonresponsiveness.
- ○ Accommodating: One stakeholder sacrifices their needs for the benefit of others.

3. Facilitator's Role

The facilitator ensures discussions remain productive by:

- ○ Preventing personal attacks and maintaining professionalism
- ○ Emphasizing shared goals over differences
- ○ Generating alternatives before deciding on a solution
- ○ Using best practices and standards to support decisions

4. Collaboration Contexts

The negotiation's efficiency is influenced by the stakeholders' physical and temporal proximity:

- ○ Same Place, Same Time: The ideal scenario for collaboration, commonly seen in Agile methodologies
- ○ Same Place, Different Time: Useful for studies requiring reflection and analysis
- ○ Different Places, Same Time: Typical of offshore teams, this requires tools like video conferencing to bridge gaps.
- ○ Different Places, Different Times: The most challenging configuration, necessitating robust tools and clear communication to manage delays and conflicts

Postnegotiation Phase

After negotiations, stakeholders are given time to reflect on the compromises and assess the impacts from their perspectives.

1. Technical Validation

Technical stakeholders can consult experts to confirm feasibility, ensuring decisions are technically sound.

2. Commitment Building

   Providing time for reflection allows stakeholders to fully commit to the decisions, reducing the likelihood of later reversals.

By following this structured negotiation process, project teams can effectively manage stakeholder expectations, align priorities, and ensure that decisions are both practical and sustainable.

Conclusion

Negotiation is a cornerstone of successful requirement management, particularly in complex projects like BI. Through prenegotiation, negotiation, and postnegotiation phases, teams can navigate diverse perspectives, constraints, and priorities to arrive at solutions that balance stakeholder interests and project goals.

This process not only facilitates understanding among stakeholders but also promotes innovation, surfaces tacit knowledge, and improves the quality of solutions through collaborative problem-solving. By incorporating techniques from conflict resolution and fostering an environment of transparency and mutual respect, negotiation becomes a powerful tool for aligning expectations and ensuring long-term project success.

Ultimately, negotiation isn't just about reaching agreements—it's about creating a shared vision and commitment to deliver solutions that meet the organization's objectives while accommodating the needs of all stakeholders. In a nonmature environment negotiations are done on reports, in more mature ones on business processes or even goals.

Quality Assurance

Traditionally, quality assurance is associated with implementing solutions, commonly referred to as "testing." However, in this chapter, quality assurance is examined from the perspective of requirements rather than development (scripts or platform installations). While rarely applied during the requirements phase, quality assurance at this stage ensures that objectives and requirements are logical, free from ambiguity, and aligned among stakeholders.

Research shows that correcting a bug during the implementation phase is up to 100 times more expensive than addressing the same issue during the elicitation phase. Poor or inadequate requirements are the leading cause of project failures, with 40 percent of software development issues traced back to subpar requirements management.

Problems with requirements can have significant impacts:

- On the solution side: Issues such as architectural flaws, design and code errors, testing difficulties, or maintenance challenges can arise.
- On the business side: Misuse of the solution, wasted time, and inaccurate decisions based on flawed data are common consequences.

Requirement Quality

Achieving high-quality requirements means producing documentation and explanations that strike a balance: being detailed enough to meet the need but avoiding excessive complexity that offers no additional benefit during implementation (Figure 2.13).

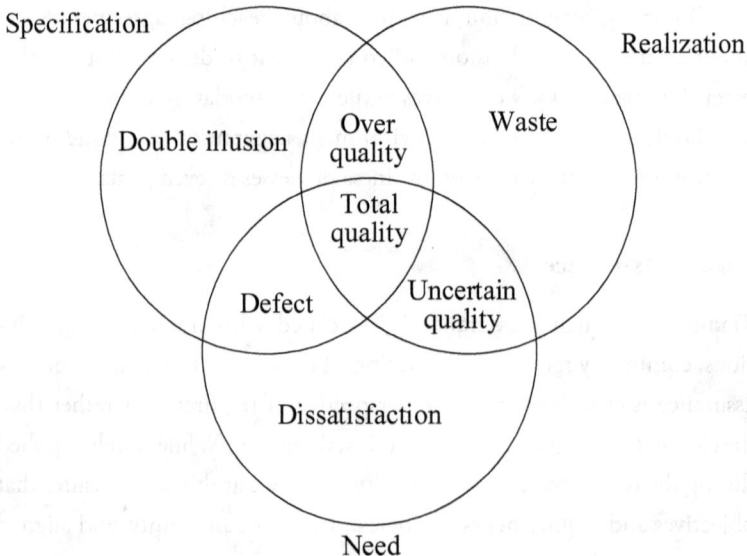

Figure 2.13 *Quality schema*

A high-quality requirement should meet several key criteria. According to the IEEE standards for requirements management, requirements should be:

1. Precise: Clearly describe the expected behavior of the solution.
2. Unambiguous: Avoid multiple interpretations by ensuring clarity. Techniques such as syntax and grammar analysis can help (see Chapter 3, Syntax and Grammar Analysis section).
3. Complete: Provide sufficient detail, including functional and nonfunctional aspects, technical descriptions, expected behavior, limitations, interfaces, service level agreement (SLA) details, process workflows, glossaries, and metrics definitions.
4. Consistent: Align with other requirements without contradictions and respect project constraints, including technical standards, good practices, budget, and security.
5. Verifiable: Allow measurable evaluation to confirm whether the requirement is met.
6. Modifiable: Be structured for easy updates and changes when needed.
7. Traceable: Clearly link back to the origin and context of the requirement for validation.
8. Prioritized and Volatile: Include priority levels and indicate the likelihood of changes, aiding in scope and change management.
9. Comprehensible: Be easily understood by all stakeholders.
10. Doable: Be achievable within the project's constraints of budget, time, and resources.
11. Appropriately Granular: Provide the right level of detail. Overly broad requirements can lead to ambiguity, while excessive detail can overwhelm stakeholders and increase management costs."

Though achieving perfection in requirements is challenging, regular review against these characteristics can improve quality significantly. Various techniques and activities can further enhance requirements evaluation.

Quality Assurance Strategies

The definition of "quality" varies by context. A quality assurance strategy should consider factors such as resources, risks, project planning, and organizational support. The strategy establishes when and how quality assurance methods should be applied and their scope.

Key considerations include:

- Available Resources: Time, budget, and expertise influence the choice of methods.
- Project Context: Legal projects often demand stricter requirements than those with flexible outcomes (e.g., forecasting with a 10 percent margin of error).
- Risk Assessment: High-risk requirements warrant higher quality assurance to mitigate potential consequences.
- Realistic Planning: Balancing thorough review with meeting deadlines is often necessary.
- Organizational Support: Established guidelines and expectations for acceptable quality levels must align with project goals and methodologies (e.g., agile vs. waterfall).

Organizations may default to constructive (proactive) or reactive (analytical) quality assurance methods. In most industries the reactive approach is preferred.

Constructive Strategies

Constructive (or proactive) methods aim to minimize errors during requirements elicitation and specification. These strategies focus on ensuring that requirements are intelligible, complete, precise, and variable early in the process. Preventative measures help reduce the likelihood of errors propagating into subsequent phases.

Reactive Strategies

Reactive (or analytical) methods verify requirements to identify and correct errors. These methods aim to prevent errors from cascading downstream and affecting other project layers. Techniques range from simple reviews to supervised quality assurance and, in some cases, semiautomated or fully automated solutions.

The main goal of reactive strategies is to limit the impact of errors, minimizing the number of affected components and associated costs. Additionally, these methods enable knowledge transfer among stakeholders, as developers and analysts can discuss and refine requirements collaboratively.

One of the most efficient and cost-effective reactive techniques is inspection, which involves four key steps: planning, detection, collection, and correction. Additional steps, like validation, may be added for complex or highly interdependent requirements.

Detection is the cornerstone of the process and can be carried out in various ways:

- Simple reading by analysts or developers to raise questions
- Stakeholder review to validate requirements from diverse perspectives
- Using a checklist based on the "5 W's" (Who, What, When, Where, Why—and, optionally, How) to ensure completeness and clarity
- Scenario-based review to assess if requirements meet user or developer needs

While theoretical, fully automated tools for quality checks exist. These systems compare requirements against predefined rules, glossaries, or dictionaries to identify ambiguities. Although these tools are costly and require formalized requirements, they demonstrate the potential for improving requirement quality.

Conclusion

Quality assurance in the requirements phase is a vital yet often overlooked process. By applying constructive and reactive strategies, organizations can reduce errors, minimize downstream impacts, and ultimately save time and resources. Whether through proactive techniques to prevent issues or reactive measures to address them, ensuring high-quality requirements is essential to project success.

CHAPTER 3

Business Analysis Applied to BI

Requirement gathering lies at the heart of every successful BI project. It is the critical first step in ensuring that solutions are tailored to meet the specific needs of stakeholders while aligning with organizational goals. This part explores a comprehensive suite of techniques designed to elicit, validate, and document requirements effectively applied in BI.

From foundational approaches like interviews and workshops to advanced methodologies such as the Goal Tree, Data Vault, and Enterprise Knowledge Development (EKD) frameworks, this section presents tools that cater to varying project contexts and challenges. Each method is evaluated for its strengths, limitations, and optimal usage conditions, providing practical insights for analysts and stakeholders alike.

It also emphasizes the importance of balancing technical and functional perspectives, navigating social dynamics, and adapting to organizational cultures. It discusses the nuances of communication, abstraction, and stakeholder alignment, all of which are pivotal in bridging the gap between business objectives and technical implementations. By the end of this section, readers will be equipped with the knowledge to select and apply the most appropriate techniques for their specific projects, ensuring clarity, alignment, and success in BI initiatives. Authors also encourage readers to mix techniques and try new ones.

Business Analysis Techniques

This chapter explores various approaches to collaborating with stakeholders in organizing and gathering requirements from a business perspective. There is no one-size-fits-all solution; the choice of method depends on the specific context, the people involved, their experiences, and the company culture. The analyst must select the most suitable techniques, weighing their advantages and limitations based on the situation. Figure 3.14, a comparative table, provides a summary of the strengths and weaknesses of each approach.

Workshop

Workshops are among the most popular methods for collaborating with stakeholders and collecting information. To maximize their effectiveness, proper preparation is crucial.

Types of Workshops

There are several types of workshops, each suited to specific goals. Below are the three main types:

- Functional Workshops
  These workshops aim to define business needs, establish priorities, and determine scope. The audience typically includes stakeholders from various business areas, with technical experts involved in a consultative role. Outcomes may include scenarios, process models, or goal trees, Post-It board.
- Technical Workshops
  These workshops focus on solving technical challenges and involve participants with diverse technical expertise, such as architects, developers, security experts, and modelers. While the discussion is primarily technical, functional representatives or analysts should participate to ensure alignment with business needs.
- Workshops Based on Functional Scenarios
  These workshops blend functional and technical collaboration, structured in three stages:
  1. Functional teams prepare a scenario or case study for analysis.
  2. Technical teams consider potential solutions for the scenario.
  3. Both teams collaborate to select and refine a solution.
  This approach allows stakeholders to interact directly while minimizing inefficiencies.

Preparation

The success of a workshop relies heavily on thorough preparation. Key elements include:

- Clearly Defined Topic
  The topic should be neither overly specific nor too vague. Stakeholders must have a clear understanding of the subject to prepare adequately or decide whether to delegate attendance.
- Optimal Group Size
  Workshops are most effective with five to eight participants. Fewer participants may limit diverse perspectives, while larger groups can hinder decision making.
- Defined Outcomes
  Stakeholders should understand how the workshop's results will be used to ensure relevant contributions.
- Logistical Planning
  Consider whether the workshop will be in-person or virtual. For in-person sessions, arrange for a suitable venue with required resources like whiteboards or conferencing equipment. For virtual workshops, ensure reliable technology and communication tools.
- Appropriate Duration
  Tailor the workshop's length to the complexity of the topic and the number of participants. Schedule breaks to maintain productivity, especially for longer sessions.

During the Workshop

Some key elements to consider during the workshop:

- Facilitation
  The facilitator introduces participants, ensures everyone has a voice, maintains the schedule, and mediates discussions.
- Time Management
  A designated timekeeper monitors progress and reminds participants of time constraints to keep the session focused.

- Decision-Making Techniques
  To resolve prolonged debates or reach consensus, consider the following methods:
  1. Voting: A straightforward approach, possibly supplemented with a veto system for legal or technical issues.
  2. Point Allocation: Stakeholders distribute points among features to prioritize them.
  3. Six Thinking Hats Method: Participants adopt different perspectives (facts, emotions, risks, benefits, creativity, and organization) to foster balanced discussions and avoid conflict.

After the Workshop

A session evaluation can be organized. The aim is to collect feedback using surveys or open-ended questions to identify areas for improvement. This step is particularly important if additional workshops are planned.

Advantages

Some advantages of workshops are:

- Facilitates Collective Intelligence
  Workshops encourage consensus-building and shared understanding among stakeholders with diverse viewpoints.
- Minimal Training Required
  Facilitators need little to no specialized training, as participants are generally familiar with the format.
- Knowledge Sharing
  Functional stakeholders can explain business challenges, while technical teams can clarify constraints, fostering mutual understanding.

Limitations

The three main limitations of workshops are:

- Scheduling Challenges
  Coordinating the availability of stakeholders can be difficult, particularly if travel is required or sessions span multiple days.

- Technology Barriers
  Virtual workshops may face issues such as poor connectivity, diffi-
  culty in real-time collaboration, and challenges identifying speakers.
- Participation Imbalance
  Some participants may hesitate to speak, while others dominate
  discussions, potentially skewing outcomes.

Optimal Usage Conditions

Workshops are most effective for addressing well-defined problems
and fostering collective solutions. Proper preparation is essential to
their success. For enhanced productivity, workshops can be paired with
complementary techniques such as scenarios, the Delphi method, or
interviews.

Interviews

Interviews are among the most widely used individual methods for
gathering information. This technique appeals particularly to those
who enjoy detective work, such as solving mysteries or uncovering hidden details.

Overview

In this approach, the analyst conducts separate interviews with stakeholders, typically face-to-face or online. These conversations can range
from informal chats to structured, form-supported interviews or directed
discussions.

To ensure unbiased results, the interviewer must practice active listening and observe participants carefully. Below are three key strategies for
successful interviews:

- Free Talk
  Allow the interviewee to speak freely without interruption. This
  approach often provides a broad overview of the topic, followed
  by critical details. The interviewer should document the discussion as accurately as possible.

- Open Questions
  Use open-ended questions to guide the conversation toward essential points. For example, ask, "Could you elaborate on that topic?" or "What are your thoughts on …?"
- Specific Questions
  Ask targeted, often closed-ended questions to confirm details. For instance: "Are you currently using these KPIs?"

The 5W2H Method

Originating in ancient philosophy and widely applied in journalism, the 5W2H method (Who, What, Where, When, Why, How, How Much) is an effective framework for structuring interviews. It can help the analyst describe a fact comprehensively:

- Who: Identifies the owner, actors, or subjects involved. Derived questions might include, "Who is responsible?" or "Who will use it?"
- What: Defines the objective, result, or item of focus. Follow-up questions might be "What is the desired outcome?" or "What resources are needed?"
- Where: Determines the physical or domain-related location (e.g., where sales occur or data is stored).
- When: Establishes timeframes, such as, "When did it start?" or "Until when is this valid?"
- How: Explores procedures, techniques, or materials. For example, "How is this process executed?"
- How Much: Quantifies KPIs, metrics, or other numerical data. Questions may include "How much budget is required?" or "How many units are impacted?"
- Why: Examines motivations and causality, helping identify the underlying problem or stakeholder motivations.
- What For: Captures the purpose or strategic alignment of the need, connecting it to broader organizational goals.

This method is particularly useful for developing functional data models and linking business needs to technical solutions. If the project involves business transformation, consider applying 5W2H to both the current and desired future states. Using complementary approaches, such as the Brown Cow model or EKD frameworks, can enhance this technique (Figure 3.1).

	Actually	In the future
Who		
What		
Where		
When		
How		
How much		
Why		
What for		

Figure 3.1 5W2H Matrix

Advantages

The three main advantages of the 5W2H approach are:

- Independent Feedback
  Each stakeholder can express their views individually, ensuring diverse perspectives are captured without group influence.

- Flexibility
  Interviews are effective for framing high-level project objectives, understanding stakeholder problems, and gathering operational details.
- Inclusivity
  In multicultural contexts or hierarchically imbalanced settings, interviews provide a platform for quieter or less influential stakeholders to share their input. This feedback can later be incorporated into group discussions to amplify their voices.

Limitations

- Potential Bias
  The interviewer must remain neutral and clarify assumptions to avoid introducing bias.
- Time-Intensive
  Conducting individual interviews for numerous stakeholders can be impractical, particularly in large projects.
- Lack of Collective Intelligence
  Interviews do not encourage brainstorming or collaborative problem-solving. Issues may only surface later in the project, potentially increasing costs.

Given these limitations, interviews should not be used as the sole elicitation technique but combined with other methods to provide a more holistic view.

Optimal Usage Conditions

- Complementary Techniques
  Combine interviews with other elicitation methods to enhance overall effectiveness.
- Limited Stakeholder Pool
  Use interviews when the number of stakeholders is manageable.
- Granularity Balance
  Questions should strike a balance between being too generic (which may yield vague answers) and overly detailed (which may overwhelm the respondent).

Delphi Method

The Delphi method is a structured, procedural approach that may take time to execute but often yields excellent results.

Overview

The Delphi method aims to separate ideas from their originators, ensuring each concept is evaluated on its merits, free from bias or preconceived judgments about the person proposing it. This technique is particularly valuable for remote teams or groups experiencing conflict, as it facilitates consensus-building on priorities and themes.

The process consists of several key steps:

1. Define the Subject
   Clearly and precisely outline the topic to ensure participants understand the focus and remain engaged. A well-defined topic prevents confusion and sustains motivation.
2. Select Stakeholders
   Identify participants with the necessary expertise, impartiality, and diverse perspectives. Including a range of viewpoints enhances the robustness of the results.
3. Create the Questionnaire
   Develop a structured questionnaire with clear and specific questions that address the topic effectively.
4. Distribute the Questionnaire
   Share the questionnaire with stakeholders, asking them to independently list their needs or priorities. Participants submit their responses anonymously to the analyst for review.
5. Analyze and Synthesize Responses
   The analyst reviews the responses to eliminate ambiguities, anonymize contributions, and group similar requirements into themes while preserving the original intent:
   - Disambiguation: Address ambiguities in the responses by clarifying concepts and ensuring precision. Common issues include one word being used for multiple concepts or several

terms describing the same idea. The analyst's domain expertise is crucial here.

- ○ Anonymization: Remove identifying details to ensure ideas are considered independently of their authors. Care must be taken to maintain granularity and precision, although this may sometimes require consolidating terms (e.g., grouping "clients," "customers," and "users" under a single label).
- ○ Summarization: Combine similar or overlapping needs into categorized themes, ensuring the summarized versions remain faithful to the original ideas.

6. Prioritization

Send the refined list of requirements back to stakeholders for prioritization. This step may include weighting participants' input based on their roles or the importance of their contributions (e.g., funding levels, market share representation). Prioritization methods might include point allocation or percentage-based ranking. Clear instructions are critical, particularly regarding weighting logic (see Chapter 2, Prioritization: A Critical Phase in Requirement Management section).

This iterative process can help refine needs further and establish precise priorities. For instance, stakeholders might initially identify the most critical parts of a process, such as onboarding new customers. Subsequent iterations could focus on specific activities within that process, asking stakeholders to evaluate success factors, such as reducing customer churn, increasing revenue per customer, or shortening process time.

Advantages

The Delphi method offers several benefits:

- Reduced Bias and Political Influence
  By anonymizing contributions, this method minimizes the impact of personal relationships, hierarchical structures, and political stakes during the elicitation phase. In hierarchical

organizations, junior employees or less influential stakeholders may feel hesitant to express their views in front of senior leaders. The Delphi method levels the playing field.
- Impartial Prioritization
  It is particularly effective for refining priorities, ensuring an unbiased and efficient outcome.

Limitations

While effective, the Delphi method has some challenges:

- Analyst Expertise and Effort
  The process relies heavily on the analyst's domain knowledge and attention to detail. The analyst must accurately classify and synthesize requirements while minimizing errors. Involving multiple analysts can help validate interpretations and improve outcomes. Tools such as syntax analysis (covered later in this chapter) can aid the disambiguation process.
- Divergent Responses
  Without clear organization, the method may result in overly divergent or nonoverlapping responses. A well-defined topic is crucial to avoid such pitfalls. This method is most effective when the project has already been established and the initial questionnaire is well constructed.

The Delphi method is a powerful tool for navigating complex or contentious projects. While it demands effort and expertise, its structured, unbiased approach fosters productive collaboration and effective decision making.

Brainstorming

Brainstorming is an effective method for fostering creativity and generating innovative ideas. It's still difficult to organize in order to get a quality output.

Overview

Brainstorming is particularly useful in situations where creativity is required. In BI it can be use in different contexts. For example, when data collection is challenging, such as measuring social or environmental impact, evaluating risks, or analyzing sentiments. It is especially helpful when dealing with external processes where data may be nonexistent, unreliable, or costly to obtain.

A brainstorming session typically includes three phases:

1. Preparation

   Define the objective of the session clearly. The organizer can stimulate participants' creativity by sharing inspiring materials beforehand and ensuring logistical arrangements, such as whiteboards, Post-it notes, pens, or other tools. Invitations should be sent in advance to allow participants to prepare.

2. Idea Generation

   Participants share as many ideas as possible, focusing on quantity and variety without judgment. The facilitator ensures that all ideas are received, encourages participation from everyone, and prevents criticism. Creative techniques like exaggeration or building on others' ideas are encouraged. The goal is to allow participants to feel comfortable sharing even seemingly absurd suggestions.

3. Idea Selection

   Ideas are organized and prioritized using various methods such as voting, assigning points, or using stickers. Prioritization should focus on the best ideas, which are then captured and documented. Key takeaways should be summarized and shared with participants, along with details of selected and unselected ideas. This step also sets the stage for subsequent phases of the project.

Brainstorming sessions are often short, lasting 30 minutes to an hour. Groups of up to 10 participants are recommended to ensure everyone has an opportunity to contribute. Diversity in participants' perspectives, experiences, and knowledge can enhance the quality of the ideas generated.

Alternative Brainstorming Techniques

The typical brainstorming described above can also be adapted as:

1. Brainwriting
   Participants write their ideas on paper (or digital documents) and pass them to others, who then add their suggestions. This technique works well for remote teams, as it doesn't require everyone to be in the same room.
2. Mind Mapping
   Create a visual map of ideas and their connections, classifying them as primary or secondary. Relationships between ideas can be labeled (e.g., "complementary," "contradictory").
3. Anti-Brainstorming
   It's based on neuroscience. Human brains are better to destroy and quantify risk than building things. Participants list unacceptable or worst-case ideas as answers to the question. This playful and counterintuitive approach can unlock creativity by flipping bad ideas into productive ones. For instance, to encourage blood donation, a session might brainstorm ideas like "acting like vampires" or "collecting menstruation blood." These absurd ideas could inspire creative campaigns, such as "Donate blood and get a free Halloween club ticket, and a campaign targeting men: "your wife gives blood 12 times a year to create life, give three times to save some."

Advantages

- Encourages Creativity
  Brainstorming is ideal for identifying functional needs and exploring alternative solutions.
- Promotes Collective Intelligence
  The technique fosters active listening and collaboration, making all participants feel valued.
- Uncovers Innovative Solutions
  When well organized, brainstorming maximizes group synergy and can reveal out-of-the-box ideas.

Limitations

- Logistical Challenges
  It can be difficult to bring stakeholders together in one place, especially for remote teams. Virtual sessions may lack the spontaneity and collaborative energy of in-person meetings.
- Facilitator Dependence
  The session's success hinges on the facilitator's ability to encourage participation and avoid judgment. Negative comments or behaviors from senior participants can stifle creativity.
- Unsuitable for Some Topics
  Topics with strict constraints (e.g., legal, security, or architecture issues) may not lend themselves to brainstorming.

Optimal Usage Conditions

Brainstorming is best suited for problems that lack obvious solutions and have minimal constraints. Establishing a trusting environment is essential. While brainstorming is commonly used to define functional requirements, it is less suitable for technical specifications.

Design Thinking

Design thinking is a user-centered, creative problem-solving approach designed to anticipate and address user needs by stepping into their shoes.

Overview

Developed by Rolf Faste at Stanford University in the 1980s, design thinking initially consisted of seven steps: define, research, ideation, prototyping, selection, implementation, and learning. Today, it is commonly structured into four key steps: understand, define, develop, and deliver, collectively known as the "double diamond" model.

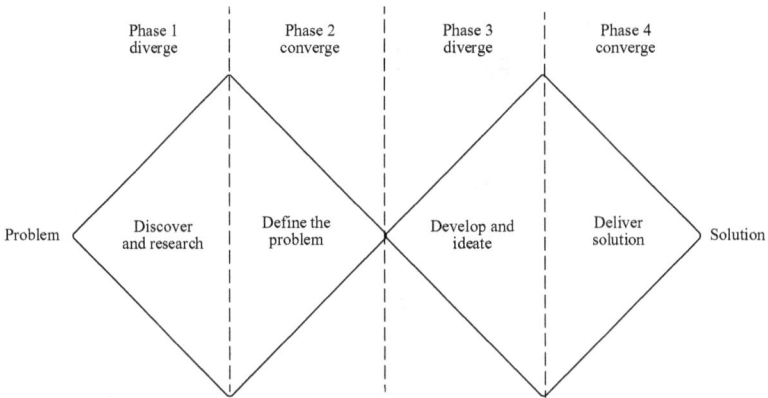

Figure 3.2 Double diamond process

The double diamond framework is divided into two distinct parts: problem definition and solution development. Each diamond consists of two phases:

1. Divergent phase: Focused on broad exploration and information gathering
2. Convergent phase: Centers on narrowing down, analyzing, and refining information (Figure 3.2)

The First Diamond: Understanding the Problem

- Understand Phase:
  The process begins with interviewing primary users to understand their needs, daily activities, and frustrations. The focus is on exploring past and present experiences rather than future solutions. For instance, identifying inefficiencies in a sales team's workflow—such as excessive time spent compiling reports—can guide the inquiry. (See Interviews section of this chapter.)
  This phase represents the divergent phase of the first diamond.
- Define Phase:
  Next, the gathered information is analyzed, sorted, grouped, and prioritized. The team defines the core functional need,

determining which problem to solve, for whom, and to what benefit. For example, the team might prioritize saving time for the sales team by focusing on specific tasks with significant impact, such as preparing client-ready reports. Prioritization is often guided by a cost-benefit analysis.

The Second Diamond: Developing the Solution

- Ideation Phase:
  In this divergent phase, participants generate as many ideas as possible without considering feasibility. Techniques like brainstorming or anti-brainstorming are ideal (see Brainstorming section of this chapter). For instance, solutions to save time might include condensed reports, audio versions of reports, or changes to the report refresh mechanism.
- Prototyping Phase:
  The focus shifts to drafting and testing one or more solutions in real-world scenarios. For example, creating an audio version of reports may emerge as the most inclusive and time-saving option, allowing users to access information while commuting or multitasking.

  Empathy is key in this phase, as understanding users' behaviors and frustrations is essential for success.

Design thinking is particularly valuable for defining KPIs. For instance, a trader aspiring to be recognized as "Financial of the Year" in the specialized press might prioritize KPIs aligned with metrics such as the largest annual bonus, highest profitability, or consistent performance. These metrics ensure the solution aligns with user goals and motivations.

Since design thinking stems from the design world, it often involves visual and interactive tools, such as Post-its, colored markers, whiteboards, and graphics. Interviews and prototyping are frequently integral components.

Advantages

Design thinking offers several benefits:

- User-Centric Approach: Places the user at the center, addressing emotions and frustrations before solution design begins.
- Balanced Process: Combines creativity with structured methodology, emphasizing both the problem and solution phases. It's avoiding to jump to solutions to quickly (Figure 3.3).
- Iterative Improvement: Observing users interacting with products (e.g., visualizations or reports) reveals areas for clarification and enhancement, leading to greater engagement and understanding.

Limitations

Despite its advantages, design thinking has some constraints:

- Dependence on Users: Requires active participation from end-users, making it unsuitable for scenarios focused on platform selection, data workflows, or enterprise architecture

Figure 3.3 Superman trying to save the world

- Challenges with Constraints: Difficult to implement in contexts with strict legal, security, or standardization requirements

Optimal Usage Conditions

This approach is best suited for designing interfaces, KPIs, or reports that directly engage human users. It is particularly effective when users can be involved in both problem identification (first diamond) and solution design (second diamond).

Thermometer Method

The thermometer method, inspired by the research of Professor S. Nurcan from Paris 1 Panthéon Sorbonne University, is a practical and engaging technique frequently employed in operational reporting projects. Its strength lies in its simplicity and the ability to provide meaningful insights into business processes. By defining clear success criteria and monitoring deviations, this method enables stakeholders to refine their processes effectively. Having applied this approach extensively, I can attest to its utility in a variety of contexts.

Overview

This method focuses on operational processes by defining what success looks like for specific activities. The developer or analyst identifies KPIs that represent successful outcomes. Any deviations from these criteria prompt further review or investigation by the business team. In essence, this method allows the analyst to "take the temperature" of each activity and engage in detailed discussions about performance and improvements.

To implement the thermometer method, the analyst models the business process, identifies key events, and associates each activity with two types of thermometers: an external thermometer for high-level monitoring and an internal thermometer for diagnosing anomalies. While this chapter describes the application of thermometers to business processes, it does not delve into process modeling techniques, as those belong to operational system modeling rather than the scope of this discussion.

Implementation Steps

The first step in applying the thermometer method involves defining the key activities within a process. Functional stakeholders, such as process managers or steering committees, decide which activities require monitoring. This decision might also involve collaborative techniques like the Delphi method to ensure diverse perspectives are considered. For example, in a phone line connection process, the business might identify three key activities: the client placing an order, the operational team installing the line, and the operational team activating the line. These steps represent critical milestones in the overall process (Figure 3.4).

Next, technical and functional stakeholders collaborate to identify the IT systems supporting these activities. Each activity may rely on none, one, or multiple systems, which might be complementary (both support a part of the business process) or concurrent (both support the same instance of the business process, the data is visible in both sources). It is crucial to identify all sources of data, even those not initially integrated into the design, as they can improve data quality or serve future needs. For

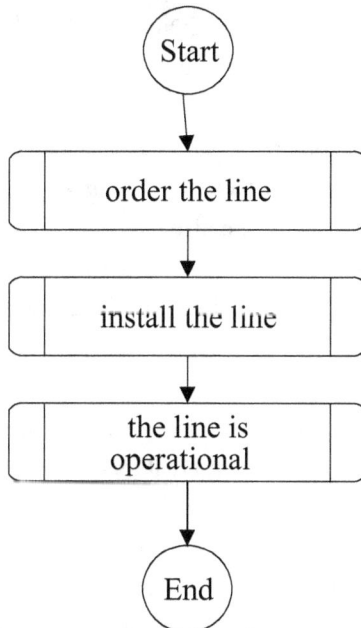

Figure 3.4 Phone line installation process

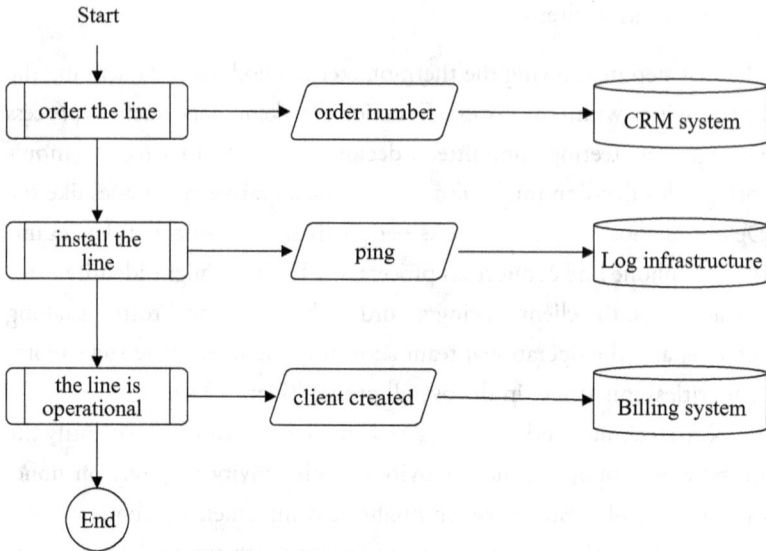

Figure 3.5 Phone line installation process with operational systems supporting the process

example, in the phone line connection process, the CRM system supports the order placement activity by creating an order number, the installation activity is verified through a connectivity test, and the activation is confirmed by the creation of a client number in the billing system to meet legal requirements (Figure 3.5).

The external thermometer provides a high-level overview of whether an activity is proceeding as expected. It focuses on answering the question: "If everything works as intended, what should happen?" For example, the external thermometer for the "line installation" activity might check if a ping from the installed line exists in the reference system, if the address matches the phone number, and if the installation occurs within five days of the order (Figure 3.6).

In contrast, the internal thermometer dives deeper into the reasons behind failures identified by the external thermometer. This step typically involves the process manager, who refines the criteria for identifying issues. For instance, if the "line installation" activity fails, the internal thermometer might identify reasons such as no recorded ping, a mismatch between the address and phone number on the installation day, or delays exceeding the defined timeframe (Figure 3.7).

meets acceptance criteria
CRIT1 AND CRIT 2 and 3

all the rest

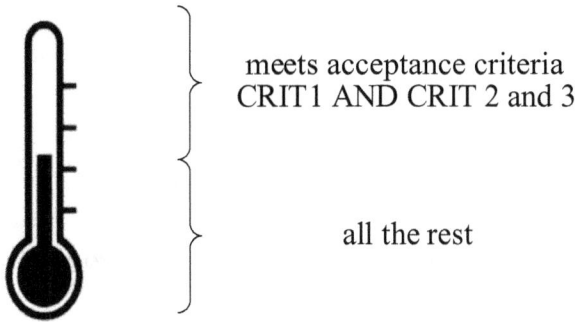

Figure 3.6 External thermometer

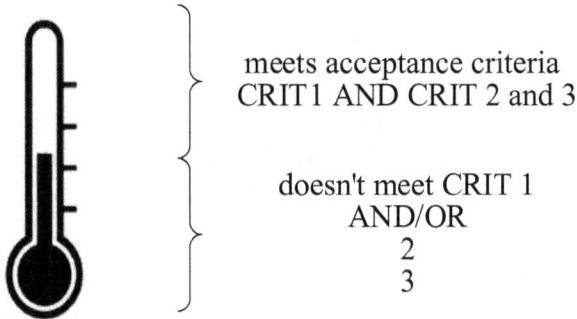

meets acceptance criteria
CRIT1 AND CRIT 2 and 3

doesn't meet CRIT 1
AND/OR
2
3

Figure 3.7 Internal thermometer

The iterative nature of this process is crucial. As process managers investigate and resolve issues, they refine the internal thermometer to reflect their findings. For example, an initial KPI might define success as a match between the address and phone number on the installation day. However, if investigations reveal that the address updates in the system with a one-day lag, the KPI can be adjusted to allow for this delay. This refinement ensures more accurate measurements and focuses attention on genuinely problematic areas.

Advantages

The thermometer method simplifies the requirement gathering process by starting with a clear model of the business process. This upfront work reduces the effort needed to define requirements during the project. Additionally, the visual nature of the method resonates well with functional users, who are often familiar with modeling their processes. Centering conversations around the business process enhances efficiency and serves as a powerful communication tool.

This approach is also well suited to agile methodologies, as its iterative process allows stakeholders to continuously refine their functional and technical definitions based on new insights. Furthermore, it supports prototyping by enabling developers to produce initial versions of operational reports even when access to users is limited.

Limitations

Despite its advantages, the thermometer method has some limitations. As it is primarily focused on operational processes, it does not guarantee alignment with broader organizational strategies. Pairing it with a goal tree can address this gap by linking operational activities to strategic objectives.

Data governance is another critical factor. Effective data governance ensures that stakeholders can make informed decisions, particularly when defining KPIs. For the external thermometer, involving a broader group of stakeholders impacted by the activity is essential, while the internal thermometer can be defined solely by the process manager to streamline decision making.

Optimal Usage Conditions

The thermometer method is most effective in contexts where business processes are well documented and understood. It excels in operational projects where iterative refinement and stakeholder collaboration are prioritized. By focusing on both high-level monitoring and detailed diagnostics, this method ensures that organizations can address issues effectively and continuously improve their processes

Collaboration Group

The collaboration group approach emphasizes replacing traditional hierarchical structures with an organic, communication-focused way of working. Its foundation lies in the belief that collective intelligence within a group is more effective than decisions made solely by a manager. By fostering open communication and multiplying information exchanges, this approach aims to uncover innovative solutions. However, its success depends not only on the quantity of communication but also on its quality.

Presentation

The behavior of migrating birds provides a compelling analogy for collaboration and collective intelligence. For example, geese fly in a "V" formation to maximize energy efficiency, with each bird benefiting from the air currents generated by the one in front. This collaborative effort increases their flight distance by up to 70 percent. However, the trade-off is reduced speed, as a single bird can fly 24 percent faster than the group. Similarly, cyclists in races often draft behind one another to conserve energy.

This concept is encapsulated in the African proverb: "If you want to go fast, go alone; but if you want to go far, go together."

In a collaboration group, all participants are collectively responsible for achieving results, pooling their resources and knowledge to meet objectives. Unlike traditional setups, there is no designated manager; instead, all team members are treated equally, and tasks are shared among them.

The distinction between cooperation and collaboration lies in task allocation. In cooperation, tasks are assigned to individuals with defined responsibilities. In collaboration, tasks are not strictly assigned, and collective problem-solving takes precedence. Here, the group's collective intelligence outweighs individual contributions.

Collaboration groups rely on three key prerequisites:

1. Proximity: Team members should work in close physical proximity, such as an open workspace, to enable direct interaction and facilitate communication naturally.
2. Intimacy: Trust must be established among team members to encourage productive discussions and foster openness. Each member should feel approachable.
3. Permissiveness: Encouraging relationships beyond the work context, such as social activities or shared leisure spaces, strengthens team cohesion and builds rapport.

However, for collaboration to succeed, individual motivation is essential. Team members must be genuinely driven to collaborate, which requires a management style that avoids competitiveness and fosters a supportive environment. Challenges may arise with high-performing individuals who may feel demotivated if their efforts are not directly credited, potentially reducing their contributions.

In the context of BI projects, collaboration groups can significantly enhance productivity. By creating multidisciplinary teams that include stakeholders and developers, decision making becomes more dynamic, and developers can easily clarify definitions and goals.

Still, this approach is not foolproof. Merely seating people together does not guarantee effective communication or uncover all constraints and needs. Prioritizing the quality of communication over sheer volume is critical.

Advantages

Collaboration groups place people at the center, creating a psychologically safe and inclusive work environment. This setting allows team members to thrive and grow.

The flexibility inherent in this approach empowers teams to allocate resources and distribute workloads based on their collective judgment, thereby optimizing outcomes. Members of the group can expand their knowledge and skills beyond their initial areas of expertise, fostering a culture of continuous learning.

Furthermore, collaboration encourages diverse perspectives, enriching the solutions developed by drawing on the varied experiences and insights of team members.

Limitations

This approach thrives in supportive and stable environments but struggles in volatile contexts where market dynamics shift rapidly or short-term objectives override long-term goals.

While collaboration fosters frequent communication, it does not inherently ensure high-quality requirements gathering or the delivery of superior solutions. Without attention to communication quality, the process may falter. That said, this method still improves team dynamics, communication effectiveness, and opportunities for learning.

Optimal Usage Conditions

To maximize the benefits of collaboration groups, it is best to combine this approach with traditional requirement-gathering techniques. A supportive and approachable management style is essential, as is mutual trust among team members. The entire team must also maintain a clear focus on the problem to be solved, ensuring that their collective efforts remain aligned with project objectives.

Use Cases and Scenarios

Business use cases and scenarios often complement one another, with use cases providing context for scenarios. While this approach is one of the simplest to implement, it can pose risks if it fails to capture the full range of possibilities and requirements.

Presentation

Ivar Jacobson first described the concept of business use cases in 1987 as "the description of the interactions between a system and its user." A use case represents a distinct and consistent feature or function within a system, typically triggered by an event. This definition underscores the role of use cases in identifying key elements of a system and its interactions.

Business Use Cases

Business use cases can serve multiple purposes, such as identifying key stakeholders, establishing data security policies, or defining business processes to capture. To formalize use cases, the process typically begins with creating a context diagram. This diagram outlines the interactions between the system under consideration and the surrounding ecosystem, which might include people, software, physical components, and time.

Each interaction within the system is then detailed as a distinct use case, initiated by an event trigger.

For example, a business use case could define roles and stakeholders:

- *"John from accounting connects to the system to verify expense reports."* This scenario identifies both a user and their specific role. Similarly, a use case might describe system interactions:
- *"The accounting system sends data to the reporting tool every Monday."* Such use cases are also helpful in defining security protocols. By outlining specific interactions between users and datasets, the business can establish access permissions. For instance:
- *"John from accounting accesses the system to review expense reports."* This implies that John needs access to the expense report table while also ensuring the accounting database supplies relevant data to the system.

Use cases can also help determine temporal dimensions of system interactions. For example:

- *"John checks the expense reports only at the end of the fiscal year."* This indicates that annual data refreshes might suffice for such reporting needs.

Furthermore, business use cases can guide the identification of data sources. By tracing recorded events back to their business origins, analysts can ensure that reports are aligned with the actual events, not merely the technical processes recording them. For example:

- If a sale occurs on Monday but is recorded on Wednesday and loaded into the system on Saturday, the report should reflect the sale date (Monday), not the recording or processing dates.

Scenarios

Once use cases and triggering events are identified, defining scenarios can add further clarity. Scenarios outline the sequential steps of a process corresponding to a specific use case. For instance:

- A scenario might describe how data flow through a system or how a user interacts with it to complete a task.

While this approach may seem comprehensive, it often struggles to encapsulate the full scope of BI requirements. Decision-making processes are rarely linear, making them challenging to model purely through user–system interactions. Using business cases and scenarios to specify a system risks oversimplification, much like attempting to design a data warehouse solely based on an exhaustive list of anticipated and predefined queries (Figure 3.8).

Advantages

The use of business cases and scenarios adopts a bottom-up approach, relying on tangible examples that stakeholders can easily articulate and developers can quickly grasp. This makes it one of the easiest methods to implement, particularly in the early stages of a project when complexity needs to be contained.

In BI, this method is particularly effective for high-level design. It is also invaluable for defining data security policies, as access scenarios can be limited to simple rules such as, "Only authorized users can access specific datasets."

	Scenario
Business event	The name of the business event triggering the scenario.
Business Case	The name and use case number of the system.
Trigger	The event triggering the scenario. It can be the arrival of data, an external request to the studied case, or a precise date and hour.
Preconditions	The conditions required for the scenario to be triggered.
Stakeholders involved	People, roles, and/or organization having an interest, knowledge, or a dependency with the scenario considered.
"Active" Stakeholders	Person, role, or organization interacting with the system.
Event 1	The list of events of the study case in the nominal scenario (if everything goes well), the alternative cases and exceptions.
[...]	
Output	The result(s) expected from the system. It can also be named postconditions.

Figure 3.8 Skeleton of a scenario description

Limitations

The primary limitation of this approach lies in the sheer number of potential scenarios, which can grow exponentially. Exhaustively identifying and documenting all scenarios can lead to scope creep and an inability to quantify project boundaries effectively. Unlike other techniques, it is challenging to apply the 80/20 rule with confidence, as critical scenarios may be overlooked.

Additionally, this method is less suited for defining data requirements, particularly when datasets are poorly understood or require significant investigation. Scenarios can, however, be useful for system design testing by providing a list of questions the system should be able to address, effectively bulletproofing the data model.

Optimal Usage Conditions

Business cases and scenarios are most effective in the early stages of a project for defining stakeholders and security policies. They can also be used to model hypothetical future scenarios, helping validate the data model's ability to support evolving business needs. By integrating these tools judiciously with other requirement-gathering methods, teams can balance simplicity with thoroughness, ensuring a robust foundation for system design.

Protocol Analysis and Apprenticeship

Protocol analysis and apprenticeship are immersive requirement-gathering techniques that allow analysts to step into the user's world. If these methods were a TV show, they might be titled *Switched!* or *The Life Swap Adventure*. These two approaches are complementary: protocol analysis captures the expert's perspective, while apprenticeship focuses on the frustrations and questions of someone new to the job.

Presentation

The essence of these techniques lies in the analyst immersing themselves in the stakeholders' environment, observing their workflows, and experiencing their challenges firsthand. The user of the future system acts as the expert or master, while the analyst assumes the role of the apprentice.

Protocol Analysis

The process begins with observation. During this phase, the analyst spends several days closely observing the users at work. This step is critical for understanding how decisions are made, identifying the most useful pieces of information, and determining the overarching goals. Observing operations also highlights which tasks are time-consuming and how data is compiled and aggregated.

This initial observation provides insights into the business processes and the key challenges faced by users. It also reveals user habits, which can inform an effective change management strategy.

Next comes the hands-on phase, where the analyst takes on the user's role. Under supervision, the analyst performs the tasks themselves, experiencing firsthand the frustrations and limitations of the existing system. This immersive experience allows the analyst to identify ambiguities, data inconsistencies, and workflow inefficiencies. Key questions often arise during this phase, such as:

- What does "number of sales" mean?
- What defines a sale?
- Why is the data inconsistent?
- What is the best data source for this task?

Capturing the analyst's first impressions and questions is crucial, as it provides valuable insights into the shortcomings of the current system.

Advantages

This technique is particularly effective when users struggle to articulate their needs or lack a coherent vision for a solution. For many stakeholders, it is easier to demonstrate what needs to be done than to describe it verbally.

Additionally, modeling requirements during the observation phase allows the analyst to gather immediate feedback, ensuring the captured needs align with user expectations.

Limitations

The effectiveness of this technique depends heavily on the analyst's ability to observe specific scenarios and generalize insights. The analyst must discern whether missing data or inconsistencies are critical or incidental.

Another limitation is that this method focuses exclusively on the existing system. While it highlights current issues, it does little to foster creativity or reimagine the solution. As a result, it may inadvertently anchor users to their old ways of working.

For example, if a user manipulates data in Excel to improve accuracy from 90 percent to 95 percent, the analyst learns that a future solution must meet a minimum standard of 90 percent accuracy, with 95 percent being ideal. However, focusing too much on existing workflows can lead to resistance to change. Stakeholders might expect the new solution to replicate the old system, viewing differences in tools, KPIs, datasets, or presentations as failures.

In some cases, the roles are reversed: The analyst is the master, and the user becomes the learner. For instance, when automating processes, a user might resist sharing their knowledge out of fear of obsolescence. In such scenarios, the analyst can train the user to develop reports or manage the database, empowering them with new skills and opportunities.

Optimal Usage Conditions

These techniques are most effective in projects with minimal change management requirements. Success depends on the analyst's ability to abstract and synthesize observations into actionable insights. Adequate time must be allocated for the analyst to immerse themselves in the environment and gather comprehensive data.

By blending the expert's perspective with the apprentice's fresh eyes, these methods ensure a deep understanding of the current system and pave the way for well-informed solutions.

Introspection

Based on neuroscience, introspection is a straightforward yet potentially powerful technique for eliciting ideas and solutions. However, it carries inherent risks if not paired with other methods. Let's explore its connection to creativity, relaxation, and those moments of inspiration that come seemingly out of nowhere—perhaps during a nap, a stroll, or even a coffee break.

Presentation

Have you ever had a breakthrough idea in the shower, upon waking, or during a casual coffee break? If so, you've already experienced the essence of introspection.

Thomas Edison and Salvador Dalí famously employed this technique, albeit with their own creative twist. Both would immerse themselves in a subject, then relax into a state of half-sleep while holding an object—Edison with a cannonball and Dalí with a key on a thread. When the object fell and woke them, they would capture the fleeting insights that emerged in this dreamy, relaxed state.

This method might sound indulgent, but it's grounded in neuroscience. The brain operates in two key modes relevant to this technique:

1. Focused Mode—This is the state of intense concentration, where a person actively works on solving a problem.
2. Diffuse Mode—This occurs during moments of relaxation or when performing everyday tasks. In this mode, the brain processes the problem indirectly, encouraging creativity and unconventional thinking.

The key to introspection is alternating between these modes. If a solution doesn't come during focused effort, stepping away and allowing the mind to wander can often yield results. Activities like walking, exercising, or enjoying a pleasant break can enhance this process, as the release of oxygen and well-being hormones boosts cognitive function.

Another form of introspection involves consulting an expert or someone skilled in modeling systems. Their fresh perspective can quickly highlight inconsistencies or new angles to consider. For analysts, simply revisiting tools or methodologies from this book can help identify potential roadblocks and spark new ideas.

Advantages

Introspection is most effective when combined with other methods from this chapter. When successful, it offers the thrill of the "Eureka!" moment—a sudden, clear insight into a problem or need.

This technique is versatile, applying equally well to functional and technical requirements. Moreover, it aids in understanding stakeholder motivations and uncovering their true drivers.

Limitations

While introspection can yield powerful results, it has to be used as a supplementary technique. It cannot guarantee outcomes within a specific timeframe and should not be relied on as the sole method for eliciting requirements.

Its unpredictable nature makes it better suited for enhancing creativity and problem-solving rather than forming the foundation of a requirement-gathering process.

Optimal Usage Conditions

Introspection is particularly useful when a situation seems stuck or when traditional methods fail to produce insights. Taking a break and allowing the mind to wander often leads to clarity. This approach is especially effective when the analyst possesses deep expertise in the domain, as their background knowledge provides a fertile ground for creative problem-solving.

By fostering creativity and leveraging the brain's natural processing modes, introspection can become a powerful tool to unlock innovative solutions and overcome challenging roadblocks.

Technical Domain Analysis

Technical domain analysis involves examining operational databases and existing systems to gather insights. While the information obtained is reliable, navigating the complexity of these sources can be challenging without a structured approach.

Presentation

Technical domain analysis is a reengineering process that aims to uncover the business rules embedded within existing systems. This involves analyzing various technical artifacts such as systems, code, SLAs, documentation, security logs, datasets, reports, and exports. Each source provides a fragment of the overall picture, requiring the analyst to piece together how the technical and business processes interact.

- Systems: Observing the architecture of interconnected systems can reveal critical details like refresh frequencies, operating hours, and system scopes. Analysts can identify upstream and downstream dependencies, where upstream systems provide input to the solution and downstream systems rely on its output.
- Scripts: Scripts often include technical definitions, active KPIs, and embedded business rules. Comments left by developers can provide additional clarity, although they may not always align with the technical documentation. In many cases, comments offer the most up-to-date insights into how the system operates.
- SLAs: SLAs are formal agreements outlining the expected performance and reliability of a system. These documents help analysts understand the criticality of databases and the architectural expectations tied to performance, availability, and maintenance.
- Technical Documentation: Comprehensive technical documentation is invaluable when building on an existing system. It can include details on data processes, constraints, business rules, and maintenance routines. Historical documentation, if available, can provide insights into how systems and requirements have evolved.

- Security Logs: By analyzing access logs, the analyst can identify who uses the data, how often, and for what purposes. This information is crucial for determining stakeholders and assessing potential impacts of changes to the system.
- Data: Datasets act as digital traces of business processes. Analysts can study these datasets to validate or challenge business rule assumptions and better understand real-world process behaviors.
- Reports: Reports showcase how data is utilized. Elements like titles, color schemes, and graphic scales can hint at underlying business rules. Filters frequently applied by users reveal focus areas, while logs associated with reports provide additional insights.
- Exports: Exported files, such as PDFs, e-mails, and Excel spreadsheets, provide key information about user needs. Frequent exports often indicate gaps in system functionality, with users resorting to external tools like Excel formulas and macros to fulfill their requirements. These workarounds often contain undocumented business rules that are vital to address in any system redesign.

Advantages

When available, technical domain analysis provides high-quality, reliable insights. Logs, code, and datasets inherently reflect the current system state, making them trustworthy sources for understanding operational realities. A quick initial review can confirm whether the information is usable, enabling analysts to proceed with confidence.

Limitations

While technical domain analysis offers valuable insights, it is not without its challenges:

- Data Gaps: Missing data, particularly historical records, can limit the scope of analysis.
- Purpose vs. Process: Technical artifacts often describe system operations without explaining their purpose or alignment with business goals.

- Resource Intensive: Fully exploring and understanding well-documented systems can be time-consuming, potentially delaying short-term project delivery.
- No Legacy System: This method is inapplicable when there is no existing system to analyze, such as in entirely new projects.

Optimal Usage Conditions

Technical domain analysis is most effective when applied to systems that are well documented, organized, and actively maintained. It is particularly suitable for projects that build upon existing solutions, where legacy systems can serve as a foundational reference.

By leveraging the strengths of this method while addressing its limitations, analysts can uncover crucial insights to inform system improvements and align technical structures with business needs. It is also useful for particular details and not the full picture.

Prototypes

Prototypes are versatile tools used to visualize and refine project requirements. By presenting a tangible representation of the solution, prototypes bridge the gap between technical teams and functional stakeholders. They are particularly effective when stakeholders struggle to conceptualize abstract ideas or when no existing solution serves as a reference.

Presentation

Prototyping involves creating one or more visual or functional models of the solution. These models help define project requirements and provide clarity on the expected outcome. Prototypes are especially useful in the following scenarios:

- When the solution is novel and stakeholders cannot picture the final product
- When stakeholders lack experience in articulating requirements or are stuck at certain stages
- When analysts or teams need to validate the project's technical feasibility

However, prototyping can be challenging if stakeholders are accustomed to a particular system. A new prototype that diverges significantly from existing processes may lead to resistance or unease about the proposed changes.

There are four main types of prototypes, each serving different purposes and contexts:

1. Conceptual Prototypes
   A simple sketch or diagram, often drawn on paper or a whiteboard, to illustrate the general layout and flow. Analysts use colored pens and visual elements to negotiate and refine ideas with stakeholders (Figure 3.9).

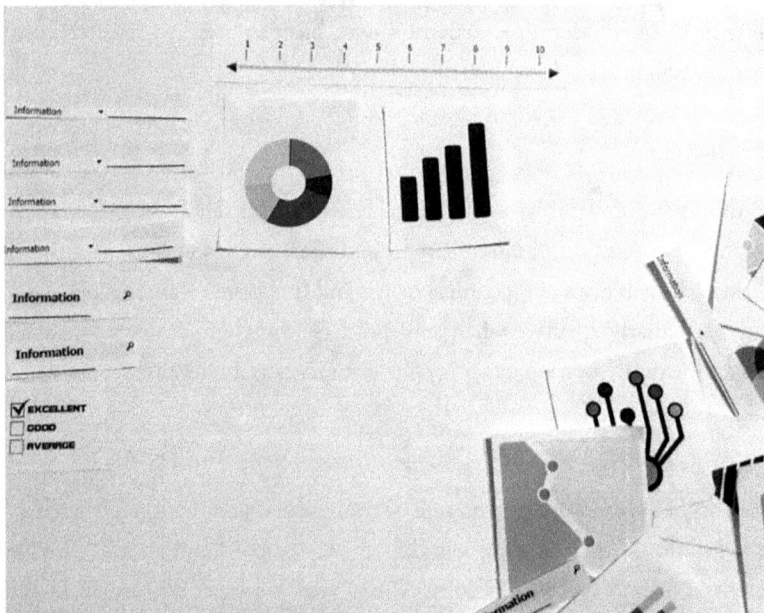

Figure 3.9 Conceptual prototype

2. Low-Fidelity (Low-Fi) Prototypes
   A more detailed version using placeholder elements like cards representing dropdown menus, buttons, or graphics. Stakeholders can arrange these elements on a mock screen to simulate interaction (Figure 3.10).

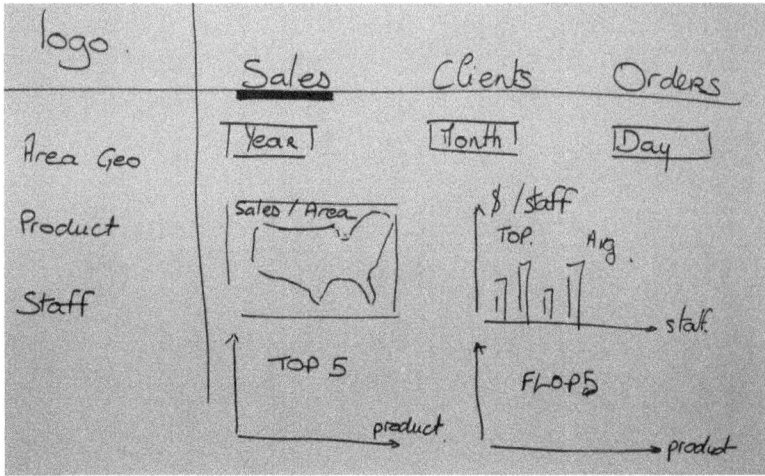

Figure 3.10 Low-fi prototype

3. Medium-Fidelity (Medium-Fi) Prototypes

   Created using software to generate screenshots or static visuals of
   the solution. These provide a closer representation of the final product's design (Figure 3.11).

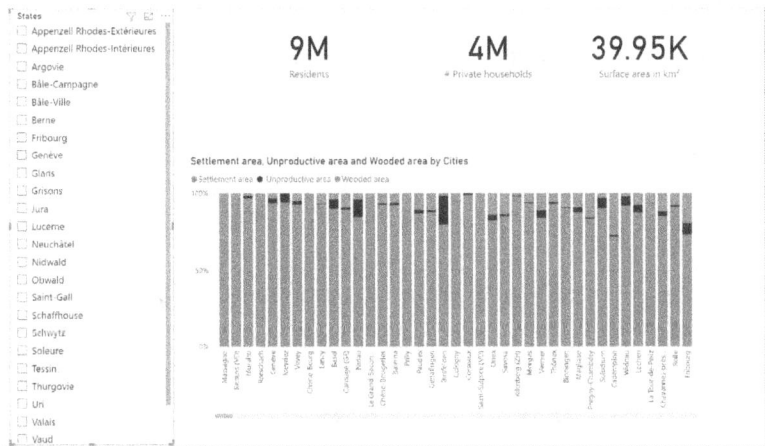

Figure 3.11 Medium-fi prototype

4. High-Fidelity (High-Fi) Prototypes

   Also called proof of concepts (POCs), these are functional models
   using real or sample datasets. Stakeholders can interact with the
   prototype to test features and validate its feasibility (Figure 3.12).

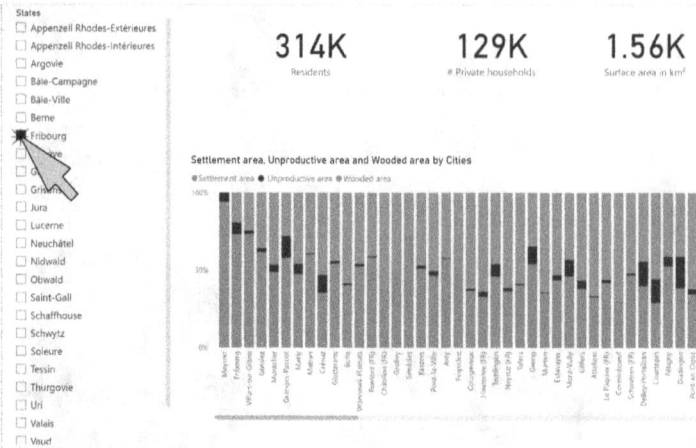

Figure 3.12 High-fi prototype

Each prototype type has its place, depending on the project's goals and stage. Conceptual and low-fi prototypes are quick to produce, cost-effective, and flexible, making them ideal for iterative discussions. Medium-fi and high-fi prototypes are more detailed and validate technical feasibility but require careful presentation to ensure stakeholders understand their scope and limitations.

Examples of Prototype Use

Prototypes are particularly valuable in scenarios such as:

- Designing dashboards to replace outdated reports during the project's initial stages
- Validating a data model by having functional and technical stakeholders collaborate on potential queries
- Addressing stakeholder impatience with tangible results by demonstrating a high-fi prototype on a clean data sample
- Building confidence during a tender process by presenting a proof of concept that showcases the technical and functional capabilities of the solution

Advantages

Prototypes offer numerous benefits:

- They validate user interface designs and technical feasibility, ensuring alignment with stakeholder expectations.
- Different types of prototypes (conceptual, low-fi, medium-fi, high-fi) provide flexibility to adapt to varying project needs.
- They enable iterative refinement and foster collaboration between stakeholders and developers.
- High-fi prototypes, in particular, build stakeholder confidence and serve as a valuable tool during tenders or project pitches.

Limitations

Despite their benefits, prototypes have limitations:

- They primarily address front-end requirements, often neglecting back-end considerations like data models, loading processes, and refresh frequencies.
- Conceptual and low-fi prototypes require a significant degree of imagination from business users.
- Medium-fi and high-fi prototypes can create confusion if stakeholders misinterpret the tool's limitations or confuse the prototype for the final product.
- Managing expectations is crucial to avoid disappointment when the delivered solution differs from the prototype due to technical constraints or scope adjustments.

Optimal Usage Conditions

Prototypes are highly adaptable and ideal for defining and validating user interface requirements, particularly in projects involving dashboards or reports. Their visual nature makes them effective tools for engaging stakeholders and refining solutions collaboratively. When used alongside other methods, such as data modeling or user interviews, prototypes ensure a comprehensive approach to requirement gathering and solution design.

Domain Analysis

Domain analysis, though often overlooked in projects, can be highly valuable and, in some cases, indispensable. It provides high-quality insights into project requirements by drawing from external standards, legal frameworks, and industry best practices.

Presentation

Before delving into domain analysis, it's essential to define the term "domain." In RE, the concept of "domain" fits into a broader categorization of "worlds," as outlined in Jarke's (1993) research. These worlds are:

1. The Usage World: This pertains to how the solution will be used in production, covering actors, stakeholders, systems, tasks, processes, and organizational politics. Functional and business requirements often originate here and are shaped by nontechnical stakeholders such as sales teams or business process owners. This world is oriented toward organizational objectives and measured outcomes.
2. The System World: This is the technical realm encompassing the specifications, platforms, databases, and architecture that constitute the product to be delivered. It represents the outcome of aligning the usage and domain worlds.
3. The Domain (or Subject) World: This world extends beyond the organization's context to include external factors like legal frameworks, industry standards, and technical guidelines. Unlike the usage and system worlds, which are influenced by organizational needs, the domain world provides foundational rules and constraints independent of internal preferences or politics.

The domain world draws on various external sources, each offering valuable insights into project requirements:

- Legal and Regulatory Frameworks: In legal or regulatory projects, requirements are heavily influenced by laws and mandates. For example, the GDPR specifies principles like data minimization and storage limitations. Depending on the context, these principles might translate into requirements for data deletion, anonymization, or restricted retention periods.
- Industry Standards: Many industries, such as retail, telecommunications, banking, and insurance, provide predefined data models and best practices. These standards serve as a reliable foundation for defining technical needs, which can then be customized for specific contexts.
- Technical Literature and Good Practices: Communities and publishers offer extensive resources on architecture, data models, and security policies. These sources are often tried and tested, providing reliable guidance.
- Software Publisher Guidelines: Vendors frequently provide benchmarks, case studies, and lessons learned from other clients. Engaging with publishers can help teams leverage established best practices and avoid common pitfalls.

Advantages

Domain analysis offers several benefits:

1. High-Quality Insights for Legal and Regulatory Projects: In such projects, domain analysis is indispensable, providing a solid foundation for requirements and identifying constraints early in the project.
2. Leveraging Community Strength: Following industry standards and community best practices ensures reliable, tested solutions. It also simplifies training and onboarding for new team members.

3. Reducing Conflict and Bias: Domain analysis shifts discussions from subjective opinions to objective references like laws, standards, and technical guidelines. This can reduce interpersonal conflicts and streamline decision making.

4. Highlighting Contradictions: This method can reveal discrepancies between organizational practices and external constraints, encouraging negotiation and alignment among stakeholders.

Limitations

Despite its advantages, domain analysis has its challenges:

- Complexity and Data Overload: It's easy to become overwhelmed by the sheer volume of information. Engaging subject matter experts (SMEs) or "translators" (e.g., lawyers, industry specialists, or technical advisers) can help navigate this complexity.

- High-Level Insights Only: Domain analysis provides an overview rather than detailed, precise requirements, making it a starting point rather than a standalone solution.

- Contradictory Information: The analyst must carefully sort through conflicting insights to identify the most relevant and actionable information.

Optimal Usage Conditions

Domain analysis is applicable to all projects and serves as a reliable source of insights. It's especially crucial in contexts involving legal constraints, industry standards, or external best practices. Analysts should leverage external expertise when necessary to interpret complex information and integrate domain constraints into the project's framing, cost estimation, and risk analysis. By understanding what has already been achieved elsewhere, teams can avoid reinventing the wheel and ensure a more efficient and compliant project delivery.

Approach by Goals

The goals-based approach is particularly well suited for BI projects. While it may initially seem complex to implement, it is highly effective for anchoring requirements, aligning the BI platform with strategic objectives, and minimizing scope creep. This method is closely related to techniques covered in Chapter 3, Modeling Languages section.

Presentation

The goals-based approach encompasses a range of methodologies for analyzing requirements through a structured hierarchy of objectives. This section provides a broad overview of the philosophy behind the approach, while specific methods such as Goal Trees, MAP, I*, and EKD are detailed in later chapters.

For clarity, we will adopt a convention for terminology: "goal" will refer to the conceptual elements of this approach, while "objective" will denote a more general or generic use of the term.

The essence of this approach is to define strategic objectives and progressively refine them into operational objectives, which in turn generate processes, scenarios, and requirements. These goals can exist at different levels of abstraction, with the highest being strategic goals, followed by tactical/management goals, and finally operational goals. Initially, the focus lies on the Usage World and Domain World objectives before addressing the systems required to support them.

Goals can be classified as either functional (hard goals) or nonfunctional (soft goals):

- Hard Goals: They are measurable and allow stakeholders to determine whether they have been achieved.
- Soft Goals: They are less definitive, often expressed as efforts to mitigate risks or achieve partial results (e.g., "minimize downtime" or "improve accessibility").

Higher-level goals are typically the responsibility of senior management, while operational goals are often automated or considered high-level requirements. Ideally, the organization's end-of-year objectives for employees align with these overarching goals.

For further detail and practical examples, refer to Chapter 3, Objectives Approach section.

Advantages

The goals-based approach offers several significant benefits:

1. Structured Engagement with Stakeholders: Analysts trained in this methodology can effectively navigate discussions with stakeholders at different levels, starting with strategic objectives at the executive level and refining them with middle management and operational teams (or sometime all the way around). This layered approach ensures clarity and alignment.
2. Revealing Overlooked Objectives: Through linguistic and syntactic analysis, analysts can uncover goals that stakeholders may not initially articulate or prioritize.
3. Completeness and Traceability: Goals help ensure requirements are comprehensive and operationalizable. They create a clear link between the organization's strategy, its operational needs, and the technical systems that support them. This traceability facilitates prioritization and reduces unnecessary scope creep.
4. Conflict Resolution and Consensus-Building: This approach helps identify potential conflicts early, allowing stakeholders to address and reconcile them before development begins. For example, stakeholders may agree to modify goals from "eliminate" to "minimize" certain risks or issues.
5. Simplified Scope Management: By explicitly tying requirements to goals, this approach makes it easier to manage scope changes and justify priority shifts. Stakeholders must align on changes to the goal hierarchy before altering development priorities.
6. Visualizing the Big Picture: Goal trees and related tools provide a roadmap that clarifies what is within the current project scope and what may fall into subsequent phases or future initiatives.

Limitations

Despite its advantages, the goals-based approach has some challenges:

1. Analyst Expertise: The effectiveness of this method depends on the analyst's skill in managing stakeholder interactions, identifying ambiguities, and ensuring no objectives are overlooked.

2. Stakeholder Agreement: Reaching consensus on terminology, goal formulation, and levels of abstraction can be time-consuming and challenging, especially for stakeholders accustomed to direct, action-oriented discussions.

3. Complexity of Abstraction: Harmonizing goals at different levels of abstraction can be difficult, particularly when using methods like goal trees or MAP.

Optimal Usage Conditions

The goals-based approach is ideal when the organization has a clearly defined strategy and its decision-making processes align with this strategy. It is particularly valuable in projects with frequent scope changes or high stakeholder turnover, as it provides a stable framework for managing priorities and maintaining focus.

This method is also useful for visualizing roadmaps, outlining future requirements, and clarifying what lies outside the current scope. By anchoring requirements to strategic goals, the approach ensures alignment and continuity, even across phases or between teams.

Syntax and Grammar Analysis

Syntax and grammar analysis is a technique designed to remove ambiguities and ensure that all stakeholders share a clear understanding of requirements. Albert Camus's observation that "to name things wrongly is to add to the misfortune of the world" underscores the significance of precise language in requirement elicitation. The method was not really used in the past, but with the advent of generative AI it is now trending.

While the technique itself has been around for decades, it has historically remained underutilized or overshadowed by more mainstream approaches in RE and business analysis. Its conceptual foundation—centered around inference, contextual interpretation, and structured language analysis—was often considered too theoretical or time-consuming for practical application in fast-paced projects. However, the emergence of generative AI has reignited interest in this method, transforming it into a critical asset for modern business analysts.

Generative AI platforms, such as large language models, bring unprecedented capacity to interpret ambiguity, resolve inconsistencies, and infer meaning from incomplete or informal input—capabilities that align closely with the technique's original purpose. As a result, what was once a niche or academically focused practice is now becoming a must-have skill for analysts tasked with managing complex, evolving, and often unstructured stakeholder inputs. Generative AI doesn't replace the analyst's expertise but amplifies it, allowing for more scalable, efficient, and insightful requirements gathering processes. This shift reflects a broader transformation in the field, where human reasoning and machine inference are increasingly integrated to improve outcomes across projects.

Presentation

Managing Ambiguity in Stakeholder Communication

In the context of requirements elicitation, stakeholders typically express their needs using natural language. While natural language is the default mode of communication between individuals, it carries inherent assumptions—namely, that words hold the same meaning for both parties, that contextual shortcuts will be correctly understood, and that the listener possesses the necessary business, technical, and cultural knowledge to interpret the message. However, these assumptions often fail, leading to misunderstandings that are difficult to detect yet costly in the context of RE.

Consider the phrase: "The solution should present the number of sales per client type." While it may seem straightforward, the term "sale" can vary in meaning. An accountant might interpret it as each line of an invoice, a sales manager might define it as one transaction per client, while a product manager might consider it the total units sold regardless of client count. Additionally, questions arise around special cases, such as deferred payments or subscription-based models. These disparities highlight how a seemingly simple term can yield multiple interpretations, all of which affect the design and implementation of the solution.

Due to the critical nature of ambiguity, several industries have developed formal methods to validate and refine requirements. For example,

NASA employs the SATFC framework to ensure clarity and consistency. Formal languages can help eliminate misunderstandings by explicitly defining requirements in a way that machines can interpret unambiguously. However, such precision often results in verbose, technical documents that are difficult for humans to read. Thus, while complete formalization may not be practical, raising awareness of these techniques can enhance stakeholder communication and mitigate misunderstandings.

The requirement elicitation process is inherently social and cognitive. Stakeholders possess different backgrounds, knowledge levels, and perspectives. Aligning their viewpoints is essential, particularly when they operate at varying levels of abstraction.

Sources of Ambiguity

Ambiguities can arise from lexical issues, such as:

- Synonymy, where different words describe the same concept
- Polysemy, where a single word carries multiple meanings

For instance, in a presales discussion, the term "client" might mean different things to different roles. A presales engineer might view the client as Mr. Paul, the procurement officer at Company A. A sales manager might associate the term with Miss Karen, the end-user overseeing implementation. Meanwhile, the accounting department might regard "client" as the legal entity, Company A. To resolve this, a more precise vocabulary should be adopted—e.g., replacing "client" with "procurement officer" or "contract manager"—and previous ambiguous terms should be discarded to avoid future confusion.

Ambiguity can also arise from referential confusion, often introduced by pronouns or generic phrases. Consider the sentence: "John is working with Tom. He saw his sister." Who is "he," and whose sister is being referred to? A clearer phrasing would be: "John is working with Tom. Tom saw Mary, John's oldest sister."

In some domains, especially legal or regulatory contexts, language is intentionally vague to ensure broad applicability. This further complicates efforts to derive clear technical requirements.

Managing Ambiguity Effectively

To manage ambiguity, analysts should provide adequate context, clearly define the scope of requirements, and ensure traceability—explaining the origin and justification of each requirement. Examples and testing scenarios can help reinforce understanding.

Analysts should also facilitate conversations that encourage clarity. Asking stakeholders to be explicit and precise fosters a shared understanding and builds a common project culture. When new participants join mid-project, having a written glossary or onboarding documentation becomes critical to maintaining consistency. Moreover, analysts benefit from answering newcomers' questions, as it often surfaces gaps in clarity that may have gone unnoticed.

Another important technique involves aligning definitions across business and technical teams. A single business concept should have one corresponding technical implementation—this includes its source, processing rules, code reference, periodicity, and security model.

Lastly, analysts can adopt a contrarian mindset: Could someone misunderstand or misrepresent a requirement, either inadvertently or intentionally? If so, it likely needs to be reformulated.

Formalization Through Goal-Based Modeling

Goal-oriented methods such as goal trees, MAP, and EKD, or tools like CREW l'écritoire, offer systematic approaches to clarify requirements. These methodologies enable the articulation of stakeholder goals and break them down into measurable needs.

Prat (1997) proposes a grammar-based model to formalize KPIs as goals composed of verbs and structured parameters. These parameters describe various aspects of a goal, such as:

- Object—the entity affected before achieving the goal (e.g., increase the customer basket)
- Result—the new entity created by the goal (e.g., create new sales)
- Reference—the qualifier of the target (e.g., new clients in a sales report)
- Source—the data origin (e.g., from the CRM database)

- Direction—the data destination (e.g., to the shared folder)
- Manner—how the goal should be achieved (e.g., automatically)
- Mean—the tools used (e.g., using SSRS [SQL Server Reporting Services])
- Quality—success thresholds (e.g., 98 percent data coverage)
- Beneficiary—who benefits (e.g., for the commercial manager)
- Place—physical or virtual location (e.g., on the tablet)
- Time—expected timing (e.g., every Monday before 9 a.m.)

This formalization results in clear, measurable requirements. For example:

"Create the new clients sales report from the CRM database and ad hoc files, stored in the shared folder, automatically using SSRS with 98 percent data accuracy, accessible by the commercial manager on his tablet every Monday before 9:00 a.m."

Such rigor facilitates robust system design and aligns expectations between business and IT stakeholders.

Verbs used to express transformation and change—such as *maintain, stop, improve, add, introduce, extend, adopt,* or *replace*—are especially useful when designing KPIs.

Advantages

The primary advantage of syntax and grammar analysis lies in its ability to reduce misunderstandings and ensure clarity in communication. Even when not fully formalized, this approach fosters a better understanding among stakeholders and encourages productive discussions. It also enhances the analyst's role as a unifying figure by facilitating clear and consistent communication. When used alongside other methods, such as interviews or goal-based approaches, this technique ensures that requirements are comprehensive and unambiguous.

Limitations

When applied too rigidly, this method can become frustrating for stakeholders and counterproductive. Fully formalized requirements may be difficult for human participants to comprehend. Therefore, it is essential to strike a balance between precision and usability to maintain stakeholder engagement.

Optimal Usage Conditions

This approach is best employed during or shortly after working sessions to refine and validate requirements. It is particularly useful in training sessions, where it raises awareness of potential ambiguities and improves communication practices. Encouraging stakeholders to critically assess and clarify language can lead to more accurate and actionable requirements, ultimately enhancing the success of the project.

Systemic Thinking

Systemic thinking is a versatile approach that can be applied at any stage of a project. While it is not a formalized method for defining requirements, it enhances the overall quality of the delivered solution by encouraging a holistic view.

Presentation

Systemic thinking involves perceiving the solution as part of a larger interconnected system. It emphasizes understanding the solution within its broader context, taking into account interactions between different systems, functionalities, and purposes.

Consider an example from the medical field to illustrate systemic thinking. A study by the International Monetary Fund analyzed the impact of corruption on organizational efficiency. Initially, corruption might seem beneficial at the transactional level, reducing process time. However, when examined systemically, the long-term consequences—such as increased complexity, rising demands for bribes, reputational damage, and legal risks—far outweigh the immediate benefits. This broader perspective helps organizations make strategic decisions that align with their long-term goals.

In BI, systemic thinking can similarly reveal benefits beyond the immediate project scope. For example, developers often work with limited visibility, focusing only on short-term deliverables. By considering the end goal and the broader context, teams can better align their efforts and anticipate future needs, reducing rework and increasing motivation.

Another practical application is leveraging shared interests across teams. For instance, in a fixed-line migration project, collaboration with a mobile customer retention team uncovered that issues with fixed services were driving mobile customer churn. By sharing BI developers, both teams benefited, and the project gained additional support, demonstrating how systemic thinking can build networks and align interests.

Systemic thinking also minimizes costs and risks. By considering future phases and potential extensions, teams can design solutions that are scalable and adaptable. For example, failing to account for potential legal reporting requirements during a business project resulted in costly rework when regulators raised concerns. A systemic approach could have avoided this scenario by incorporating high-level foresight into the initial design.

For systemic thinking to be effective, stakeholders must be willing to step back and ask high-level questions. It requires a collaborative environment where short-term priorities do not overshadow long-term benefits. Essays by Edgar Morin offer deeper insights into the philosophy behind systemic thinking.

Advantages

Systemic thinking significantly improves solution quality by providing a comprehensive "big picture." This perspective helps reduce redundancies and inconsistencies between project phases, ensuring smoother transitions and minimizing rework.

The approach fosters motivation and collaboration by uniting internal and external stakeholders around shared objectives. By identifying existing resources and solutions that can be repurposed, systemic thinking reduces workload and enhances efficiency.

Limitations

Despite its benefits, systemic thinking has limitations. It is challenging to anticipate every possible scenario, and teams may lose sight of organizational benefits when navigating conflicting stakeholder interests. Understanding the company's structure and dynamics is essential, which can be difficult for newcomers, contractors, or in rapidly changing environments.

Optimal Usage Conditions

Systemic thinking is most effective when resource management and long-term planning are priorities, particularly during the project's initial stages. It thrives in environments that encourage out-of-the-box thinking and provide psychological safety for exploring innovative ideas.

To implement systemic thinking successfully, the analyst must be highly engaged and curious, and stakeholders should be incentivized to think beyond their immediate responsibilities. This approach can lead to better resource optimization, stronger collaboration, and a more adaptable, future-proof solution.

Brown Cow Model

The Brown Cow model is a practical framework for distinguishing functional needs from technical requirements. It facilitates communication among stakeholders, especially in projects involving significant changes.

Presentation

At first glance, the name "Brown Cow" might seem unusual, but it holds a meaningful approach. The model uses a four-quadrant framework to separate the "What" from the "How" and the "Now" from the "Future." This structure helps delineate functional and technical requirements while steering conversations away from entrenched habits, such as "We've always done it this way." By doing so, the Brown Cow model avoids reintroducing existing system weaknesses into new solutions.

The quadrants divide responsibilities: Functional stakeholders focus on the top two quadrants, while the technical team handles the bottom two. This segmentation encourages stakeholders to think beyond their current processes and focus on the broader needs and questions the project seeks to address. For example, instead of starting with a directive like, "Load data from the sales table into the marketing cube daily," stakeholders might be encouraged to frame the problem as, "How can we verify if our targeting aligns with what customers are purchasing?"

Separating the "What" from the "How"

This distinction allows analysts to consider various implementation options. It shifts conversations to focus on solving the problem rather than prescribing a technical solution prematurely.

Separating the "Now" from the "Future"

This division emphasizes the "Why" behind transitioning from current functionalities to future ones. It ensures clarity on whether existing functionalities should be preserved, replaced, or modified. Once this analysis is complete, the "How-Future" quadrant can be described and compared to the "How-Now" quadrant to estimate the required effort, costs, and change management implications.

The technology-agnostic nature of the top quadrants allows stakeholders to assess the needs without being constrained by current technical limitations. This step forces stakeholders to justify their existing habits and evaluate whether they remain relevant in the future context.

And about the name ...

The Brown Cow model typically starts with filling the "How-Now" quadrant, tying it to the tongue-twister, "How now, Brown Cow?" (Figure 3.13)

Advantages

The Brown Cow model is straightforward to implement and effectively clarifies roles and responsibilities among stakeholders. It encourages users

Now | Future

Actual
business
cases

Future
business
cases
(improved)

What   What

How   How

Actual
features

Future
features

Now | Future

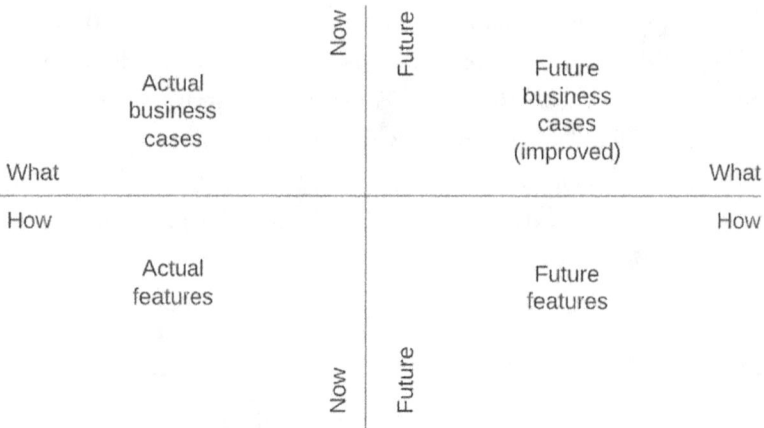

Figure 3.13 Brown Cow model

to justify their needs and routines, helping the team minimize technical debt. By reframing discussions, it fosters better alignment between functional and technical perspectives.

Limitations

This approach works best when there is a clear "Now" situation to analyze. It is not effective for entirely new projects or platforms with no existing system to compare. If the old and new systems are fundamentally different, comparing them can hinder progress; in such cases, it is better to treat the new solution as a fresh start. Additionally, while the model structures conversations, it does not inherently guarantee the quality of requirement elicitation.

Optimal Usage Conditions

The Brown Cow model is ideal for projects aiming to develop a new version of an existing solution, especially when change management is a priority. It is particularly useful in scenarios where business and technical stakeholders are unclear about their respective roles. By defining distinct scopes, the model ensures a more structured and collaborative approach to requirement elicitation (Figure 3.14).

Approach	Collective	Individual	Complexity	When to choose
Workshop	X		X	To surface a collective solution. When collaboration is easy.
Interviews		X	X	Difficult collaboration. Preliminary work required. Trained analyst.
Delphi	X	X	XXX	Difficult collaboration. Influence issues.
Brainstorming	X		X	To surface a collective solution. When collaboration is easy. Creativity required.
Design thinking	X		X	Interface definition, User experience focus.
Thermometer method		X	X	Business process well defined. Basic KPI definition. Availability challenges.
Collaborative groups	X		XX	To surface a collective solution. Easy to implement in AGILE methods.
Use cases and scenarios		X	XX	Business process definitions. Operational reporting.
Protocol analysis and apprenticeship		X	XX	Functional stakeholders have difficulty explaining needs; tacit knowledge.
Introspection		X	X	Analysis by SME; complement other approaches.

Figure 3.14 Comparative table

Approach	Collective	Individual	Complexity	When to choose
Technical domain analysis		X	XX	Existing architecture in place; understand constraints.
Prototype		X	XXX	UI visualization required; tenders.
Domain analysis		X	X à XXX	Legal constraints; standards.
Goal-oriented approach	X	X	XX	Aligning solution with strategy; manage scope; trained analyst.
Syntax and grammar analysis		X	XXX	Complement other approach; minimize ambiguities.
Systemic thinking		X	XXX	Understand impact of decisions; manage system holistically.
Brown-Cow model		X	XX	Improving existing solutions; scope not defined; change management focus.

Figure 3.14 (continued)

Modeling Languages

Objectives Approach

Requirement management is a structured process that translates informal or unspoken needs into actionable formal requirements for implementation by the data team. Although the process can often be complex and disorganized, the approach driven by objectives provides a framework that brings structure to the effort. By linking an organization's strategies and objectives to technical requirements, this approach ensures that the implemented solution aligns with the organization's overall goals.

Presentation

The objectives approaches are foundational to many IT methodologies, including EKD-CMM, KAOS, I*, and MAPS. This chapter introduces the EKD methodology, a comprehensive approach to modeling knowledge, context, and solutions. Among the EKD models, the goal tree plays a central role, serving as a key tool for organizing and understanding objectives (Figure 3.15).

Figure 3.15 Goal model, also called objectives model

At its core, the objectives approach aims to answer the fundamental "why" of a solution. The initial goals are often high-level and may stem from business, market, strategic, technical, functional, or methodological imperatives. These goals are then refined and connected to form a structured hierarchy of objectives that spans strategic, tactical, and operational levels (Figure 3.16).

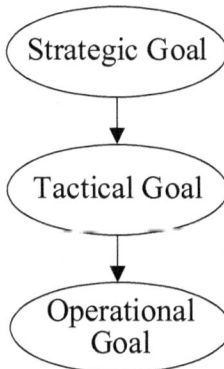

Figure 3.16 Objectives' abstraction levels

The relationships between goals can take several forms:

- Refine: One goal contributes to the realization of another, typically at a higher abstraction level.

- AND: Both goals must be achieved for the main goal to be fulfilled.
- OR: Achieving either of the linked goals satisfies the main goal.
- Conflict: Two goals cannot be achieved simultaneously due to contradictory objectives.

Goals and scenarios are often interlinked. Scenarios provide a behavioral description of the system necessary to achieve specific goals, ensuring traceability and alignment. Iterating between goals and scenarios allows for refinement, fostering completeness and coherence.

Formulating and Reasoning with Objectives

Goals can be expressed in various ways: informally, semiformally, or formally. Methods like Elektra simplify goal articulation, focusing on actionable verbs such as *Maintain, Stop, Improve, Add, Introduce, Extend, Adopt,* or *Replace.* These verbs naturally align with how users describe their needs for reports or dashboards. Advanced linguistic tools, such as those outlined in CREW l'écritoire, help eliminate ambiguities, while formal methods like KAOS offer rigorous approaches to goal formulation.

Formalizing goals not only aids in understanding but also allows for reasoning about alternatives, dependencies, and conflicts. For example, when two goals—such as "Improve the conversion rate from Prospect to Client" and "Extend client retention"—share common elements like the definition of "client," collaboration between stakeholders ensures consistency and cost efficiency. Conflicting goals can often be managed by seeking compromises or partial solutions that satisfy overarching objectives.

This structure of cascading goals enables a process called goal tree navigation. When moving down the goal tree, the analyst is answering the question "how"—how can the higher-level strategic objective be achieved through concrete actions or subgoals? Conversely, when navigating up the tree, the question becomes "why"—why is this action or subgoal necessary, and what broader organizational objective does it support? This bidirectional reasoning helps ensure that all efforts remain aligned with the company's strategy while offering clear justification for each requirement included in the scope (Figure 3.17).

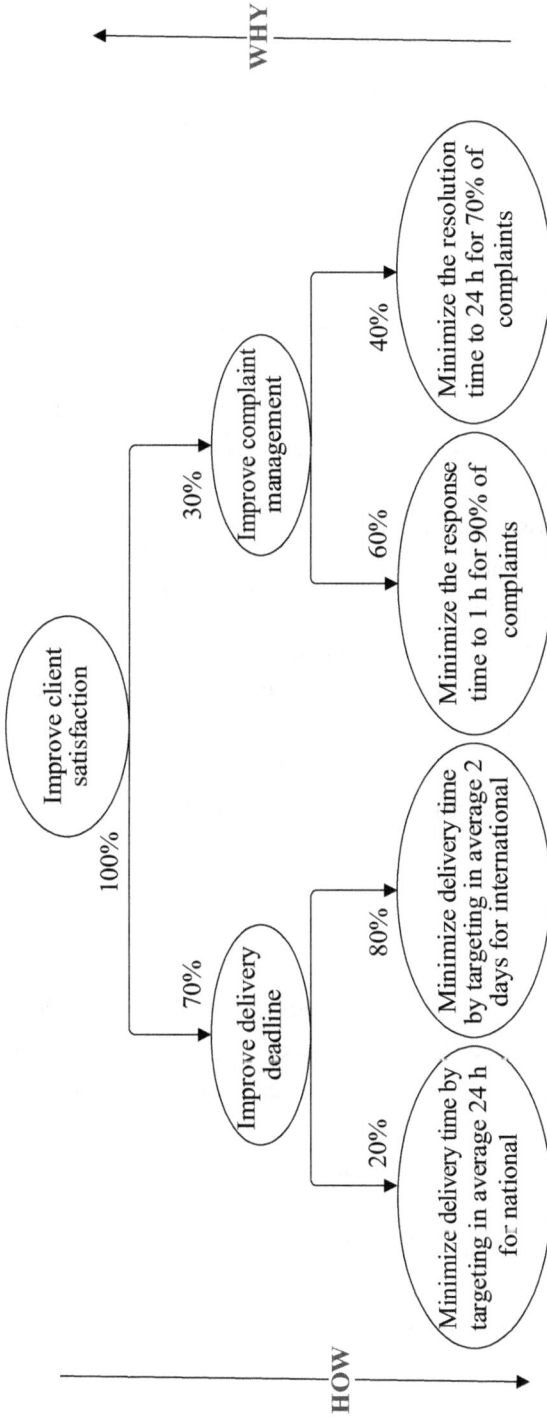

Figure 3.17 Goals tree navigation

The following example illustrates how a goal tree can be used to break down a high-level strategic objective into actionable subgoals. It shows the logical progression from a company's vision to the specific actions required at each level of the organization to achieve it (Figure 3.18).

Advantages of the Objectives Approach

The objectives approach provides numerous benefits, including:

1. Traceability: Goals are directly linked to organizational objectives and external contexts, ensuring alignment and easier change management.
2. Discovery of Alternatives: By focusing on "why," stakeholders can explore alternative solutions before committing to a specific implementation.
3. Enhanced Problem Understanding: Emphasizing the problem before the solution fosters a deeper understanding of challenges and opportunities.
4. Scope Control: Formalized goal trees help maintain project scope and prioritize changes, reducing the risk of chasing moving targets.

Limitations

Despite its advantages, the objectives approach comes with challenges. Articulating all necessary objectives can be difficult, as the process demands time, effort, and stakeholder commitment. Some may find the exercise overly detailed or redundant. Moreover, effective facilitation and stakeholder training are essential for success, especially in discovering alternative goals.

Additionally, while ideally integrated into an organization's strategy or annual plans, goals are rarely formalized this way. As a result, reverse engineering is often necessary to recreate the context and rationale behind existing systems.

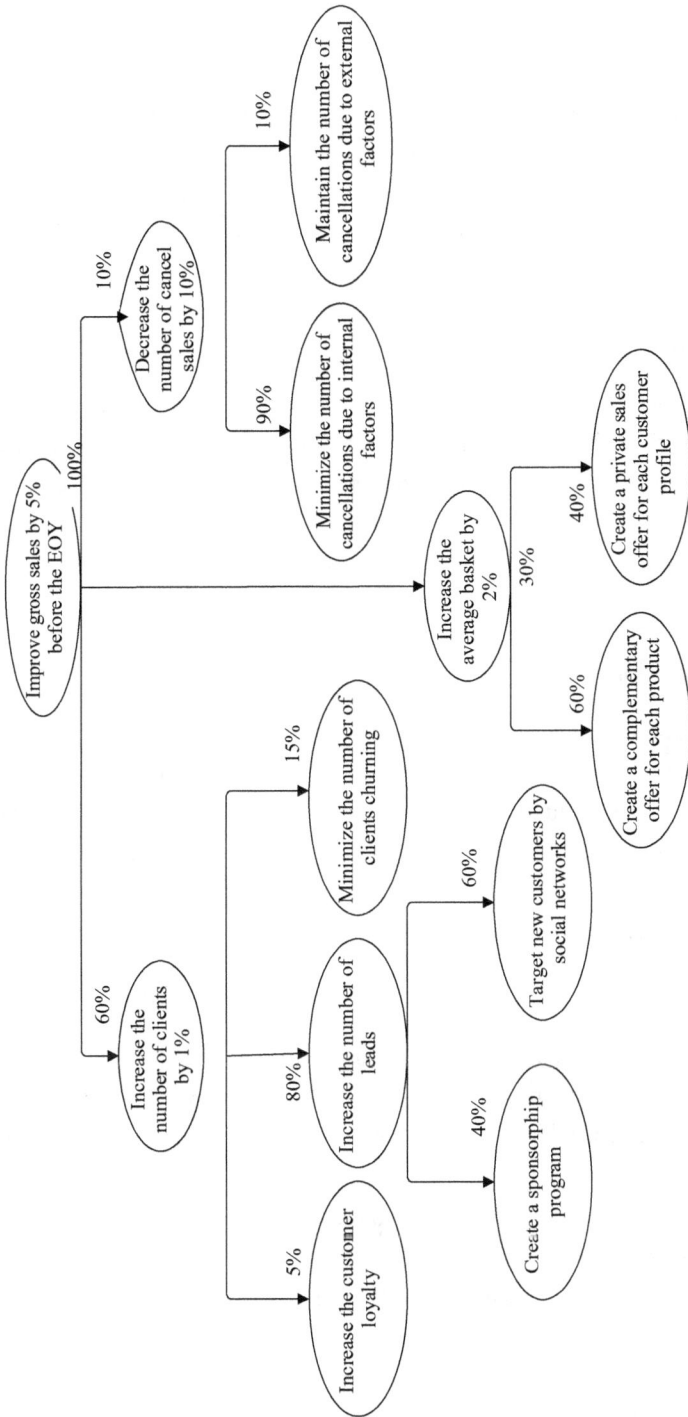

Figure 3.18 A goal tree example

Optimal Use

The objectives approach is particularly valuable when there is a clear alignment between organizational strategy and operational needs. By fostering collaboration, facilitating conflict resolution, and providing a structured framework for requirement management, this method ensures that solutions address both immediate and long-term objectives.

Ensemble Logical Model

The Ensemble Logical Model (ELM) is a framework designed to facilitate the initial stages of Data Vault implementation. Often seen as a precursor to the creation of the Data Vault layer, ELM serves as the foundation for building Kimball or star schemas, commonly used in BI solutions.

Presentation

ELM addresses the challenge of uniting stakeholders from diverse backgrounds and ensuring effective communication during the early phases of a project. The primary goal is to simplify the modeling process, enabling functional stakeholders to participate actively from the outset and remain engaged until the technical team takes over.

Originally developed for the Data Vault model, ELM consists of three main steps:

- Identify and model the main functional concepts.
- Identify and model the relationships between these concepts.
- Identify and model the contexts for the main functional concepts.

During these sessions, various tools, such as Post-its, forms, and models, are used to facilitate the process. The choice of tools depends on the project's context, the team's maturity in requirement elicitation, and the desired outcomes.

The process begins with brainstorming to identify key concepts, an activity often referred to as "facilitation." At this stage, the focus is not

Figure 3.19 Main concepts example

on creating a formal model but on generating a comprehensive list of concepts using tools like Post-its (Figure 3.19).

- Categorizing Concepts: Once identified, concepts are grouped into five categories: events, people, places, things, and other concepts. This categorization helps identify gaps and eliminate synonyms.
- Main Concepts Canvas: A canvas can be used to visually organize concepts into their respective categories. This allows the team to group related ideas and ensure that each event has associated concepts across categories. Not all events may have concepts in every category, but this method reduces the likelihood of missing key elements and elements of keys (Figure 3.20).
- Defining Relationships: The team then establishes relationships between events and core concepts. These relationships form the "backbone" of the data model (Figure 3.21).
- Attributes and Contexts: In the final step, attributes and contexts for each concept are defined, further enriching the model and setting the stage for development (Figure 3.22).

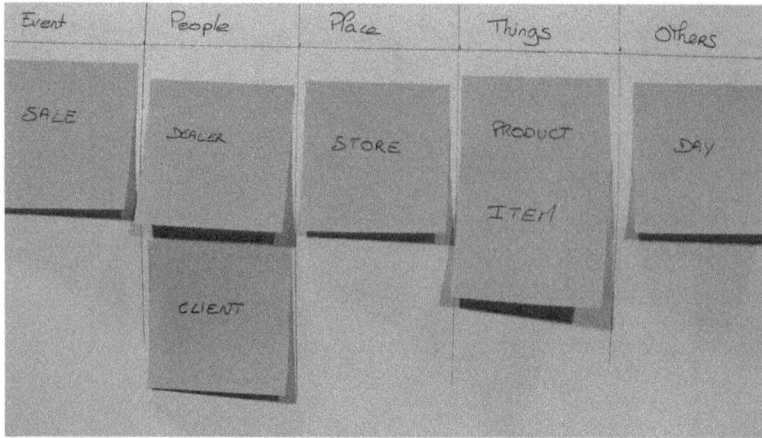

Figure 3.20 Main concepts categorization

Figure 3.21 Definition of links between core concepts

Advantages

The ELM approach offers several benefits:

- Clear Separation of Conversations: By distinguishing between technical and functional discussions, ELM reduces communication barriers and frustrations arising from differing stakeholder cultures and perspectives.

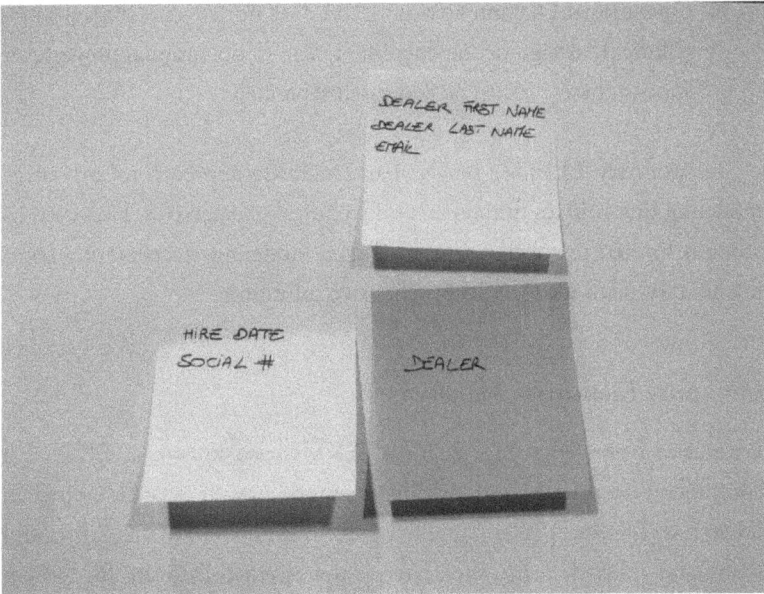

Figure 3.22 Definition of attributes and contexts of the core concepts

- Active Functional Involvement: Functional stakeholders are actively engaged in designing the solution, fostering collaboration and shared ownership.
- Iterative Development: ELM supports an incremental approach to data warehouse projects. It does not require complete modeling of all business processes before development begins, enabling quicker project starts and iterative refinements.

Limitations

While ELM is an effective tool for creating the Data Vault layer, it has certain limitations:

- Dimensional Layer Support: ELM provides guidance for the Data Vault layer but only offers indirect insights into the dimensional layer of the data model.
- Strategic Guidance: The method does not address the "why" behind decisions or help in establishing priorities.

- Operational Documentation: ELM does not cover technical architecture design or the documentation of operational processes, leaving these areas to be addressed separately.

In summary, ELM is a practical and inclusive approach to early-stage modeling that bridges functional and technical perspectives. However, its scope is limited to specific aspects of data modeling, necessitating complementary methods for a comprehensive solution.

Enterprise Knowledge Management

Enterprise Knowledge Management (EKM), also known as EKD, is a comprehensive enterprise modeling methodology. It was developed in Sweden during the 1980s, initially by Anne Persson and Janis Stirna and PlanData's research team, then later at the Swedish Institute for System Development. EKM was pioneering in its conceptualization of "business goals" or objectives, which allowed for the first time the modeling of stakeholder and organizational intentions. This innovation made it possible to evaluate whether existing processes align with and achieve the organization's goals.

Presentation

EKM evolved until the early 2000s and has since stabilized into a structured framework comprising a language and a modeling process. The language consists of six interconnected submodels (Figure 3.23):

1. Goal Model
2. Business Rules Model
3. Concepts Model
4. Business Process Model
5. Actors and Resources Model
6. Technical Components and Requirements Model

Each of these models captures a specific aspect of enterprise knowledge. EKM has two main applications in BI projects: documenting the

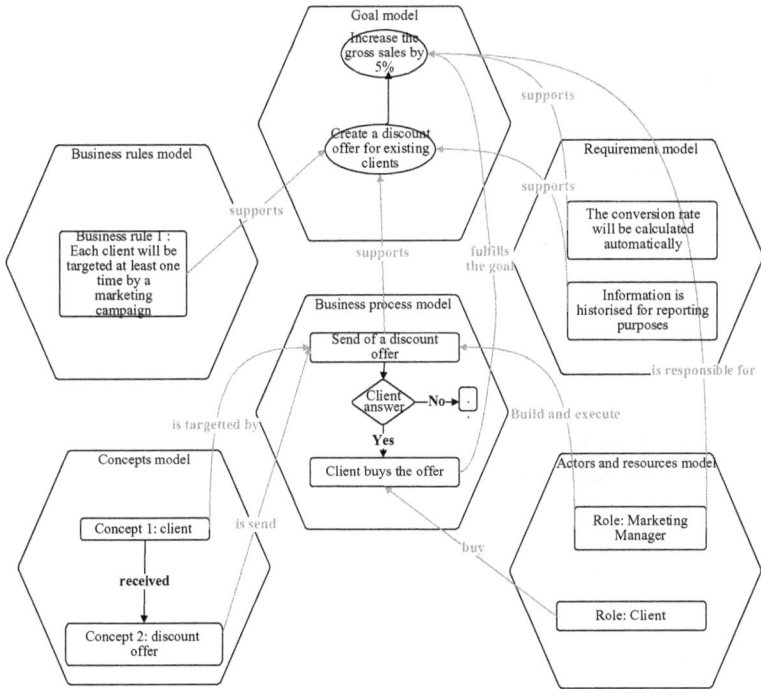

Figure 3.23 Chunk of an EKD example

project itself and documenting operational systems. While it's rare to find perfectly documented operational systems when starting a BI project, EKM provides a framework for identifying missing information, assessing risks, and guiding the requirements gathering process.

To understand how EKD fits within a BI initiative, it is helpful to first consider the various information sources that feed into a BI solution. The following diagram illustrates these sources, highlighting the role of structured modeling approaches like EKD in connecting strategic objectives with operational data (Figure 3.24).

The Goal Model

The goal model describes the objectives of the organization and its stakeholders, distinguishing between goals that should be achieved and those to be avoided. It establishes a hierarchy of goals, linking operational

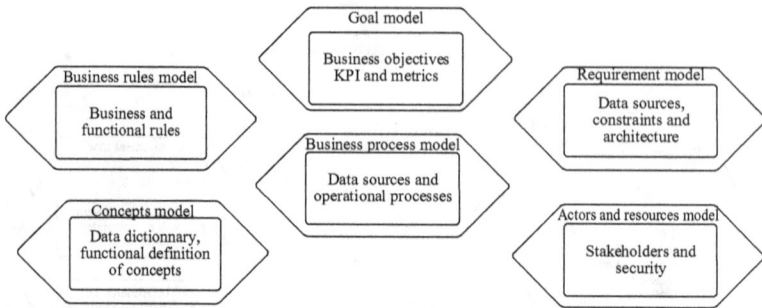

Figure 3.24 What are the information sources of a business intelligence solution?

objectives to tactics and overarching strategies. Key questions addressed by the goal model include:

- What are the organization's priorities?
- How do different goals interconnect?
- What pitfalls should be avoided?

In BI, this model helps define metrics for each objective, ensuring alignment between organizational goals and the BI activities.

The Business Rules Model

This model captures functional rules derived from the goal model, representing operationalizable goals. It defines existing practices and rules, addressing questions such as:

- What practices are in place to achieve goals?
- What are the rules affecting these goals?

In the context of BI, this model helps define processes for data access, upgrades, self-service, and report creation. For operational systems, it aids in understanding business rules and defining data exceptions.

The Concepts Model

This model defines the key concepts used within the organization. It serves as a communication foundation, avoiding ambiguities and inconsistencies. It includes definitions, exclusions, and implementation details, addressing:

- What are the key concepts, and how are they defined?
- How do these concepts integrate into the BI solution?

In operational projects, this model documents data models, layers, schemas, and platforms. For BI, it includes a data dictionary that bridges functional and technical stakeholders.

The Business Process Model

This model outlines the organization's business processes and the data required for each activity. It connects processes with goals, addressing:

- How are tasks and processes accomplished?
- What data is required for each activity?

For BI, this model documents data access, transformation, and quality issues. For operational systems, it links objectives, processes, and priorities, highlighting data sources and quality concerns.

The Actors and Resources Model

This model identifies actors and resources, linking them to goals and processes. It answers:

- Who is responsible for each objective and process?
- How does the organizational structure impact the project?

In BI, it identifies users, developers, and maintenance personnel while detailing physical resources like servers and software. For operational systems, it clarifies stakeholder roles, data escalation, and security policies.

The Technical Components and Requirements Model

This model focuses on technical specifications, including architecture diagrams and data models. It answers:

- What technical requirements must the solution satisfy?
- Which components support specific objectives and processes?

In BI, it documents platform components, data warehouse layers, urbanization, predefined reports, and client applications. For operational systems, it provides alternative data sources and technical insights.

The EKD Process

EKD does not prescribe a rigid process for creating these models, thus allowing for flexibility in execution. A participative approach is recommended, emphasizing collaboration among stakeholders. The facilitator's skills in modeling, conflict management, and mediation are critical for success. EKD also includes an extension for change management (Enterprise Knowledge Development–Change Management Method [EKD-CMM]) to support evolving business needs.

Advantages

- Comprehensive Coverage: EKM captures both technical requirements and broader enterprise context, offering a holistic view of needs.
- Traceability: The methodology emphasizes linking developments to organizational objectives, making it easier to understand the rationale behind each component.
- Alignment with Goals: By documenting business processes and objectives, EKM ensures that BI activities align with organizational priorities.
- Improved Communication: The structured models enhance communication between functional and technical stakeholders, minimizing misunderstandings.

Limitations

- Incomplete Documentation: Perfectly documented operational systems are rare, requiring analysts to address missing or imprecise information.
- Collaboration Requirements: Success depends on a collaborative environment, which may be challenging to achieve in some organizational cultures.
- Time-Consuming: The significant upfront effort required for modeling can be a challenge in agile project environments.

Optimal Usage Conditions

EKM is ideal for projects where a comprehensive understanding of enterprise knowledge is essential. While it may be challenging to implement in fast-paced or poorly documented environments, it provides a robust framework for aligning technical solutions with organizational goals. By addressing gaps and risks early, EKM sets the stage for successful BI initiatives.

Unified Modeling Language

UML is a modeling language designed for creating diagrams of object- and process-oriented systems. While UML is not inherently suited for data-centric projects like BI, certain components can still be adapted to visualize and design BI systems effectively. However, applying UML in BI often requires flexibility and a loose interpretation of its structures.

Presentation

UML is not a methodology but a modeling language, meaning it provides syntax and visual elements for creating system diagrams without prescribing a step-by-step approach. These diagrams can support communication, development, and sometimes even automation by describing operational sources.

UML consists of 14 types of diagrams, divided into two main categories:

1. Structure Diagrams:
   These include Class Diagrams, Component Diagrams, Deployment Diagrams, Object Diagrams, Package Diagrams, and Composite Structure Diagrams.
2. Behavioral Diagrams:
   These encompass Use Case Diagrams, Activity Diagrams, State Machine Diagrams, Sequence Diagrams, Communication Diagrams, Interaction Overview Diagrams, and Timing Diagrams (Figure 3.25).

Adapting UML for BI Systems

Some UML diagrams, like Class Diagrams, can inspire data model definitions. For instance, while a Class Diagram typically models classes with attributes, methods, and functions, in a BI context, it can be repurposed to model tables by focusing on attributes and relationships, excluding constraints and methods (Figure 3.26).

The utility of UML in BI is limited by its origin as a tool for modeling operational systems supported by object-oriented languages like Java and C++. It is designed to define system components, actors, and behaviors with relatively fixed variability. By contrast, BI systems must support dynamic, unstructured decision-making processes, such as ad hoc data exploration or self-serve reporting, which are challenging to model with traditional UML diagrams.

For example, creating a Use Case Diagram for a self-serve reporting system would be counterproductive since users can generate a wide variety of visualizations from the data catalog, making it nearly impossible to map every potential interaction (Figure 3.27).

Practical Applications in BI

While UML is not directly suited to BI, certain diagrams can still be leveraged:

- Class Diagrams: Useful for outlining the foundational structure of data models

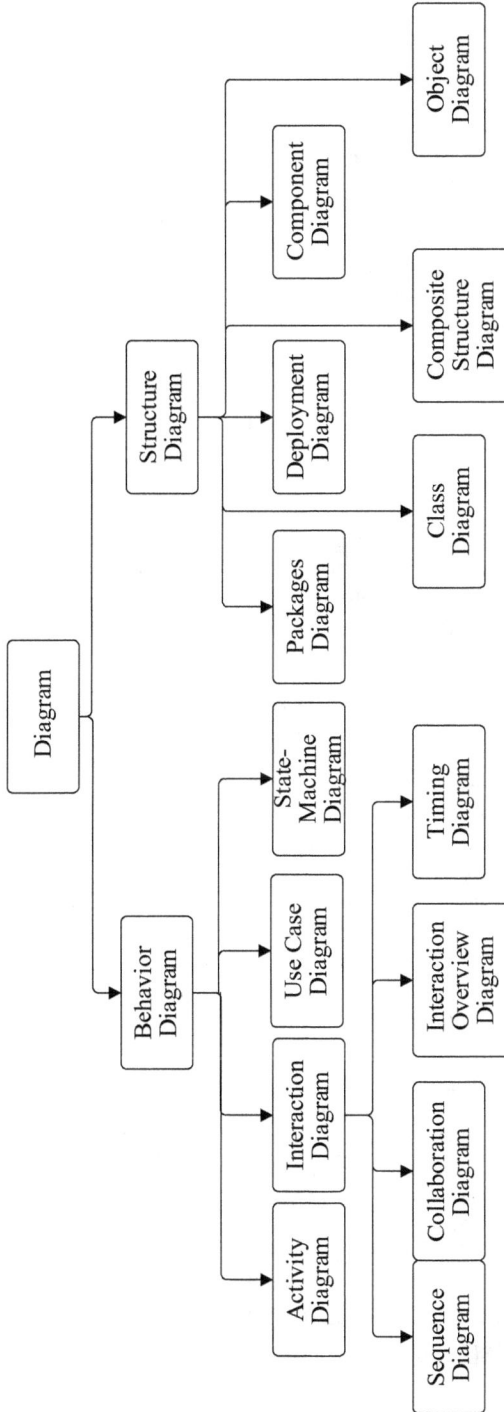

Figure 3.25 UML diagram hierarchy

Diagram	Definition	Potential BI Uses
Class Diagram	Object-oriented. Conceptual architecture of the system. Describe classes and links	Connectors for data sources, inspiration for data model (entity-relation)
Object Diagram	Illustration of a class diagram (the class diagram is a meta-model of the object diagram)	Data source connector (pointless/rarely use)
Use Cases Diagram	Main functionalities required for users/system relationship	Incident management, security, visualization tools description
Activity Diagram	Process visualization	Incident and support process management, production tables management, business process
Sequence Diagram	Chronology of the operations to be done by a user	MDM, data, and ETL automation
Component Diagram	Organization from the software point of view. Software components, data, or even configuration components	Data loads between the different layers of the BI structure, physical architecture, enterprise architecture
Deployment Diagram	Use of the physical infrastructure by the system and the way system components are organized and their relationships	In DevOps: deployment high-level
Package Diagram	Package of systems and their relationships	In DevOps: deployment low-level
Profile Diagram	Definition of a class and collaborations	Few to no use
Composite Structure Diagram	Internal actions of a class, including the relationships of nested classes, detailed	Few to no use
State Machine Diagram	Define objects life cycle	Version upgrades, operational process
Communication Diagram	Light version of the sequence diagram focusing on message transmission of the object	Data loads between the different layers of the BI structure, physical architecture, enterprise architecture
Interaction Overview Diagram	Overview of the flow of control of the interactions (sequence diagram variation)	Few to no use
Time Diagram	Representing the variation of data over time	Few to no use

Figure 3.26 UML diagram BI usages

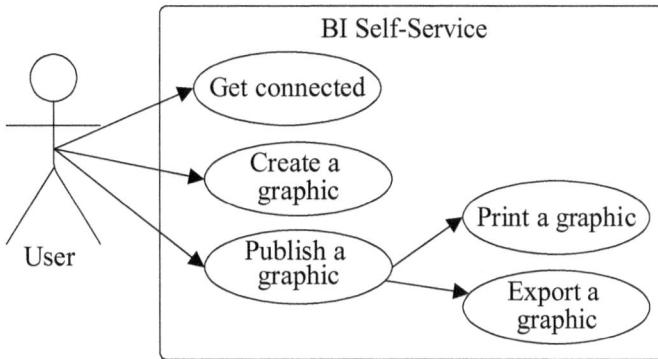

Figure 3.27 Ineffectiveness of Use Case Diagrams for self-serve reporting

- Activity Diagrams: Can help describe workflows or processes within operational systems that feed into BI (Figure 3.28)
- Sequence Diagrams: Can capture interactions between systems or components in the data pipeline.

Advantages

Even if UML is not really made for BI, a business analyst can still get some benefits out of it:

- Widespread Familiarity: UML is a widely recognized standard, familiar to both analysts and technical teams.
- Ease of Implementation: Its simple syntax and extensive tooling (e.g., Microsoft Visio, Lucidchart) make it easy to learn and apply.
- Standard for Operational Systems: As a default methodology for documenting operational systems, UML is often already in use and can serve as a starting point for BI documentation.

Limitations

Some of the main limitations of UML for BI are:

- Focus on the "How": UML excels at describing the "how" of systems—components, relationships, and behaviors—but lacks mechanisms to address the "why."

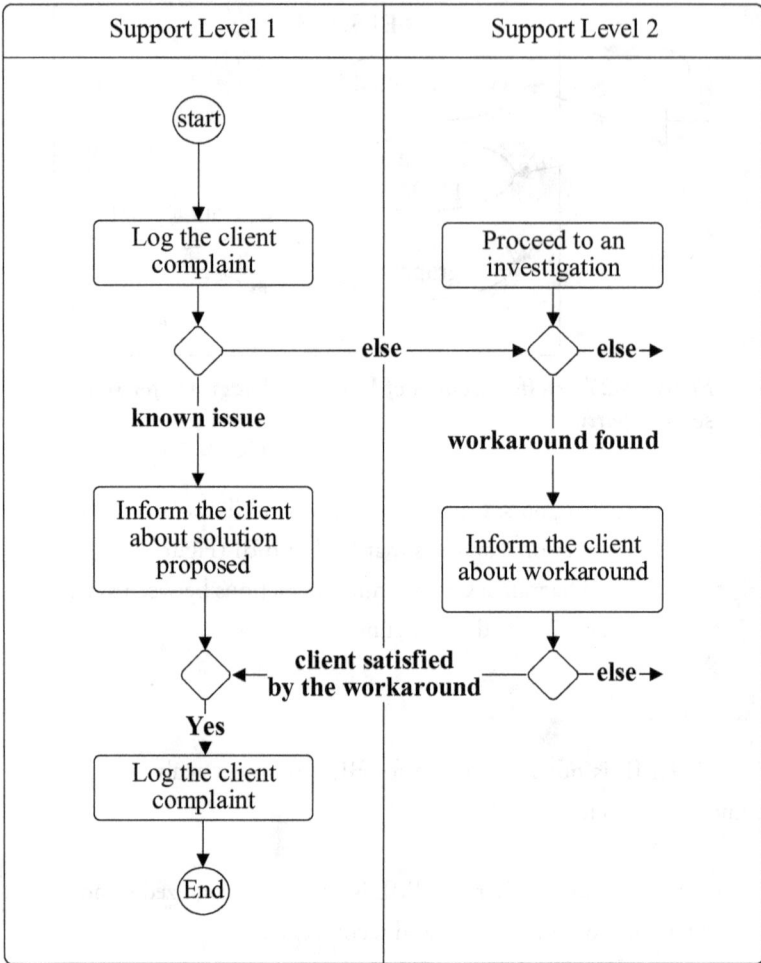

Figure 3.28 Activities diagram in UML example

- Limited Alignment with Strategy: UML does not naturally align system design with company objectives, strategies, or priorities, which are essential in BI projects.
- Ineffectiveness for BI-Specific Needs: UML struggles to model the unstructured, exploratory nature of BI tasks, such as ad hoc reporting or dynamic data exploration.

Conclusion

While UML is not an ideal fit for BI projects, certain components can still be adapted to describe processes, operational systems, and data structures.

	Utilization	Implementation Effort
UML	Diversify to document the "who." UML is a methodology oriented on operational process documentation that doesn't fit well with business intelligence project documentation. It's still possible to use it to document the business process from which the data will be captured.	Simple
Objectives approach	Document the "why" of the initiative and the priorities. It's really useful to ensure the alignment of the decisional system and the organization strategy. This approach is also interesting to limit the scope changes.	Average
EKD	The most complete documentation: objectives, business processes, architectures, security. EKD handles the documentation on all facets.	Complex
ELM	Definition of the core business concepts and their relation. Produce a specification of the data model for DataVault and a draft for the Kimball layer. This methodology is really simple to put in practice and helps to create bridges between functional and technical stakeholders.	Simple

Figure 3.29 Modelization comparison table

Its strength lies in its familiarity and simplicity, but its inability to address strategic alignment and BI-specific needs limits its effectiveness. When used in BI, UML should be applied selectively and with flexibility to support specific project goals.

Methods Comparison

Not all methods are universally applicable to every context. Each comes with its unique strengths and weaknesses, making it crucial to select the method best suited to the specific needs and circumstances of the project. By tailoring the choice to the project's context, analysts can maximize the effectiveness and value of their approach (Figure 3.29).

Particular BI Requirements

This chapter offers a high-level overview of key technical and BI-specific domains. Each topic covered could warrant an entire book on its own, but here it serves as a starting point for discussions with relevant stakeholders. The chapter will explore areas such as security, data quality, data governance, architecture, and data modeling approaches.

Security

Security in BI encompasses various aspects to ensure data protection and integrity. These responsibilities can be categorized into four main areas:

- User Authentication: Verifying the identity of the person requesting access
- Server Authentication: Ensuring users connect to the legitimate BI system, avoiding malicious impersonation
- Encryption: Protecting data transmission so that exchanges between users and the BI system cannot be intercepted
- Data Security: Guaranteeing that users can only access data they are authorized to view

User Authentication

BI systems should not handle authentication directly, as this can lead to significant security vulnerabilities. Instead, a centralized authentication system, such as Active Directory, should manage user authentication. Modern authentication relies on token-based systems, such as OAuth 2.0, which is widely adopted for its robustness.

The token-based authentication process includes the following steps:

1. The user requests a token from Active Directory with a specific access scope (e.g., BI datasets).
2. Active Directory validates the request and issues a token.
3. The user presents the token with every request to the BI system.
4. The BI system validates the token with Active Directory before granting access.

Older systems may rely on challenge-based authentication, such as NT LAN Manager (NTLM), which directly exchanges security information between the user and the BI server. However, this method is considered outdated and vulnerable, making it unsuitable for modern implementations.

Certificate Viewer: mail.google.com

General   Details

Issued To

Common Name (CN)	mail.google.com
Organization (O)	<Not Part Of Certificate>
Organizational Unit (OU)	<Not Part Of Certificate>

Issued By

Common Name (CN)	GTS CA 1C3
Organization (O)	Google Trust Services LLC
Organizational Unit (OU)	<Not Part Of Certificate>

Validity Period

Issued On	Monday, August 22, 2022 at 10:25:29 AM
Expires On	Monday, November 14, 2022 at 9:25:28 AM

Figure 3.30 Certificate example

Authenticating the BI System

The BI system must authenticate itself to users to prevent man-in-the-middle attacks, where a malicious actor intercepts and mimics the legitimate system to steal sensitive credentials.

This is achieved through certificate-based authentication. The BI system provides a certificate, verified by a trusted third-party certificate authority, ensuring the user connects to the correct system. Secure Sockets Layer/Transport Layer Security (SSL/TLS) is the standard protocol for this purpose, with TLS being the only recommended version since 2022 (Figure 3.30).

Encryption

Encryption ensures secure communication between users and the BI system. Using a certificate-based asymmetric encryption system, the BI system provides a public key to encrypt data. Only the BI system can decrypt this data using its private key. Once the data exchange begins, a symmetric key, shared securely between the user and the BI system, is used for faster encryption of the ongoing data flow.

Access Security

After user authentication, it is crucial to enforce data access restrictions to ensure users only view permissible data. BI systems typically employ:

- Row-based security: Filters data by rows to limit user access. For example, an U.S. sales manager would only see sales data for the United States.
- Role-based security: Restricts access to specific data fields based on user roles. For example, finance staff may access financial data but not HR records, and vice versa (Figure 3.31).

Country	2025 Revenue	Headcount
Australia	100,000	10
France	200,000	20
Japan	300,000	30

Figure 3.31 Example of Row-Level Security

In practice, row-based security is almost always required, while role-based security depends on the specific requirements of the organization.

Data Quality

Data quality is critical for most organizations. Implementing an effective data quality policy can significantly improve decision making and operational efficiency. This guide outlines a streamlined approach to establishing a data quality framework, helping identify common issues and prioritizing meaningful solutions. Much like rescuing a diver in distress, data quality management follows structured steps to address challenges effectively.

Awareness

The first step in addressing data quality is recognizing when and where problems exist. Similar to identifying a missing diver before initiating a rescue, identifying data quality issues requires defining what constitutes "good quality" data. This process often involves iteration, visualization, and analysis to establish benchmarks.

Common drivers for data quality policies include:

- Unpredictable Issues: Many problems only become apparent after observing anomalies, requiring creative and pragmatic solutions.
- Management Acceptance: Substantial discrepancies can shift focus from solutions to blame assignment. A clear quality policy minimizes political distractions by providing actionable insights.
- Iterative Definitions: Understanding data deviations from the ideal scenario enables stakeholders to refine quality standards over time.

A helpful tool for this phase is the "thermometer method," which supports iterative analysis and improvement, as discussed in Chapter 3, Thermometer Method section.

Assessment

Once an issue is identified, it's essential to evaluate its impact and determine the response. Similar to assessing a rescue operation's feasibility, the team must weigh the potential business and technical consequences of data quality issues.

Key considerations include:

- Stakeholder Notification: Promptly inform relevant parties, especially for production problems.
- Criticality Assessment: Evaluate whether the issue justifies immediate intervention or can be deprioritized.

- Strategic Response: Determine the most suitable approach to address the issue. For example, a bug affecting only forecast data may not warrant urgent attention, but one leading to regulatory fines would.

Strategies for managing errors may include:

- Rejecting: Exclude flawed records from datasets.
- Accepting: Acknowledge the error but take no corrective action.
- Correcting: Identify and address the root cause of the issue.
- Mitigating: Implement workarounds, such as using alternative fields or data sources.
- Applying Defaults: Use placeholders like "unknown" or "N/A" to provide interim fixes.

Action

This phase involves implementing the agreed-upon solution. After prioritizing and planning, the team proceeds to address the issue, ensuring alignment on the strategy and required effort. Clear planning minimizes the risk of pursuing low-impact fixes while maintaining focus on critical tasks.

Aftercare

Even after resolving a data quality issue, continuous monitoring is crucial. Modern BI systems and data platforms are highly complex and dynamic, so side effects or recurring bugs may arise. Establishing a monitoring system with automated alerts can preempt future problems, much like a thermometer alerts overheating in baking.

Remarks

When dealing with data quality, two key points are worth noting:

1. Dual Origins of Issues: A report or dataset always reflects two overlapping processes:

○ Business Processes: These involve activities such as sales, stock management, or workflow stages that generate data. Errors may stem from operational inefficiencies or incomplete tasks.

○ Technical Processes: These IT processes include data extraction, transformation, and loading; source system bugs or latency; and platform and network stabilities.

Separating issues by root cause—business or technical—can clarify remediation efforts and owners

2. Context-Dependent Definitions: The definition of "good quality" varies based on usage. For instance, a legal report may demand stricter criteria than an optimistic forecast.

By systematically addressing data quality through these steps, organizations can enhance trust in their datasets and ensure data-driven decisions are based on reliable information.

Data Governance

The Gartner Group distinguishes between data and information in their respective governance contexts.

- Data Governance is defined as: "The specification of decision rights and an accountability framework to ensure the appropriate behavior in the valuation, creation, consumption, and control of data and analytics."

- Information Governance is described as:

The specification of decision rights and an accountability framework to ensure appropriate behavior in the valuation, creation, storage, use, archiving, and deletion of information. It includes the processes, roles, policies, standards, and metrics that ensure the effective and efficient use of information in enabling an organization to achieve its goals.

Both definitions emphasize establishing structured decision-making processes, accountability, and compliance to enable organizations to achieve their goals effectively.

The Importance of Data Governance

Data governance serves multiple purposes, such as improving process efficiency, adhering to regulatory requirements, and enhancing customer service. According to the *Data Governance Survey 2017* by CIO WaterCooler, the primary drivers for data governance implementation are:

- Process Efficiency: Motivates 54 percent of organizations
- Regulatory Compliance: Accounts for 39 percent
- Customer Service Improvement: Represents 7 percent

Key Roles in Data Governance

A successful data governance initiative depends on contributions from multiple stakeholders, including senior executives, managers, project teams, and data stewards. Among these roles, executive sponsorship is critical. The same survey highlights that with executive support, stakeholder understanding of the value of data governance rises significantly—from 32 percent to 72 percent (Figure 3.32).

The data steward plays an equally important role. This individual ensures that governance processes and best practices are adhered to, identifies areas for improvement, and facilitates the adoption of governance practices within teams.

Advantages of Data Governance

Establishing a robust data governance framework offers numerous benefits for BI solutions:

- Improved Data Understanding: Accurately naming, tracking origins, and understanding the use of data enhances the decision-making process.
- Enhanced Data Quality: Reliable and trustworthy data improves reporting accuracy, fosters user trust, and promotes solution adoption.

● Without top management support   ◌ With top management support

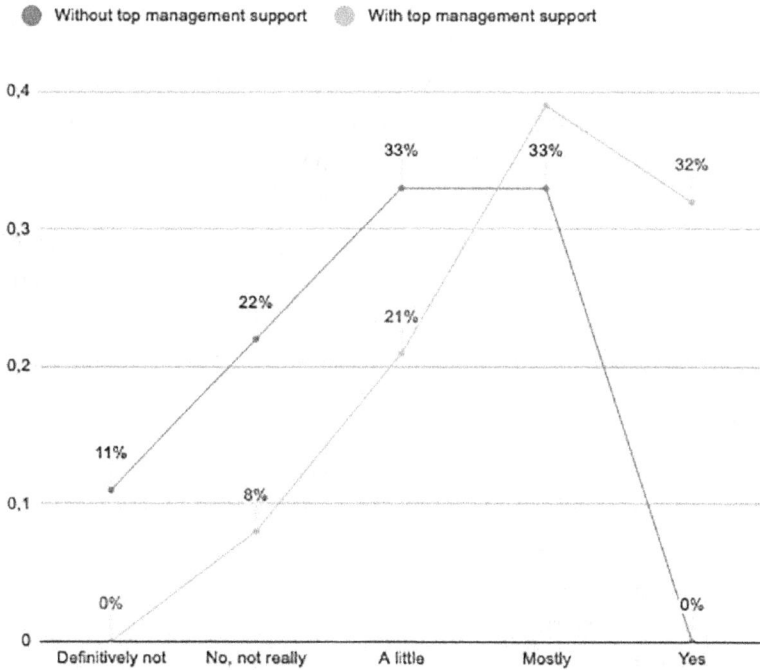

Figure 3.32 "Is the value of data governance understood by the business with and without top executive sponsorship?"

Source: Data Governance Survey 2017—CIO WaterCooler and Veritas.

- Data Mapping: Creating a comprehensive map of data sources prevents duplication of data storage, reduces development and maintenance efforts, and increases user confidence.
- Regulatory Compliance: Proper governance is often mandatory for datasets subject to legal and regulatory requirements, such as those in the banking, health care, and government sectors.
- Clear Guidelines and Best Practices: Well-defined governance rules help users and developers understand what is feasible, permissible, especially in self-service reporting scenarios.

By implementing data governance policies, organizations can streamline processes, build trust in their data, and ensure compliance, creating a solid foundation for effective BI solutions.

Architecture

Exploring the domain of architecture in its entirety would require an entire book. This chapter, while not exhaustive, highlights key considerations for making sound architectural decisions in BI projects. Thoughtful architectural planning is crucial because these choices significantly influence the solution's agility and can be challenging and costly to reverse. Additionally, existing solutions, particularly those burdened with technical debt, may constrain architectural options.

Guiding Principles for Ideal Solutions

An effective architecture adheres to several guiding principles:

1. Support for Diverse Use Cases
   The solution should accommodate a broad spectrum of use cases, including reports for senior management, predefined visualizations (such as scorecards and dashboards), analytics and predictions, ad hoc queries, OLAP (online analytical processing) cubes, and self-service capabilities. While not all use cases need to be addressed initially, the architecture should be flexible enough to support their future implementation.

2. Data Quality and Granularity
   High data quality is essential for enabling accurate decision making. Granularity should also be carefully managed. If the granularity is too high, operational reporting may lack the necessary detail. Conversely, excessive granularity can slow down reporting and increase maintenance costs.

3. Agility and Maintainability
   To ensure the solution is agile and easy to maintain, the architecture's layers must be clearly defined and thoughtfully planned. Striking a balance is critical: too few layers may reduce flexibility, while too many layers increase development and maintenance complexity.

4. User-Friendly Design
   The solution should mask complexity and offer a user-friendly experience, enabling nontechnical stakeholders to use the system effectively.

5. Data Governance and Security
Architecture should seamlessly support data governance, from data creation to centralized security, ensuring compliance and stream-lined management.

6. Guidelines and Best Practices
To prevent disorganization, the architecture should be underpinned by robust guidelines and best practices.

Additional Considerations

When planning architecture, the following factors must also be considered:

- Refresh Frequency
The required data refresh frequency—ranging from monthly or weekly updates to near real-time or per-second refreshes—has a significant impact on the choice of platform, architectural design, associated costs, and necessary optimizations.
- Component and Process Management
The architecture should plan for:
  ○ Component management
  ○ Data integration and cleansing
  ○ Business rule implementation
  ○ Semantic layers for enhanced data interpretation
  ○ Security protocols
  ○ Interoperability with other systems
  ○ At least one user-friendly presentation layer

Additionally, it must support production deployments, maintenance plans, system upgrades, and component life cycle management.

Balancing Key Concerns

All architectural decisions should weigh the trade-offs between hardware, network capabilities, and software constraints. These considerations en-sure a scalable, sustainable, and high-performing BI solution tailored to organizational needs.

Data Modeling Approach

Even if data modeling as such is more oriented toward solution and data engineering, this chapter can really help the business analyst assist developers in building the solution.

Kimball Methodology

Ralph Kimball, often regarded as the father of BI, introduced dimensional database modeling in the mid-1980s. While widely recognized for his contributions to dimensional modeling, Kimball's work extends far beyond this, offering a comprehensive approach to data warehouse construction. This chapter highlights key elements of his methodology as they relate to the themes of this book, providing insights into its practical applications.

Kimball's life cycle framework structures the process of designing and implementing a data warehouse into distinct phases. These phases guide teams through planning, requirement gathering, dimensional modeling, physical design, ETL development, deployment, and ongoing improvement and maintenance (Figure 3.33).

Data Life Cycle

Kimball's approach to managing the data life cycle involves three core activities: dimensional modeling, physical design, and ETL development.

Dimensional modeling establishes the foundation for the enterprise data warehouse. The process begins with identifying the business process to be analyzed, capturing functional problems, defining reporting needs, and profiling data with input from stakeholders. Data profiling is critical to ensure the business process is accurately represented.

Granularity determines the level of detail stored in the data warehouse. Striking a balance is essential—too much detail increases costs and complexity, while too little fails to meet users' analytical needs or future requirements, undermining the principle of a "single source of truth."

Dimensions provide descriptive attributes for facts: the context of the business event. Once the granularity of business events is established,

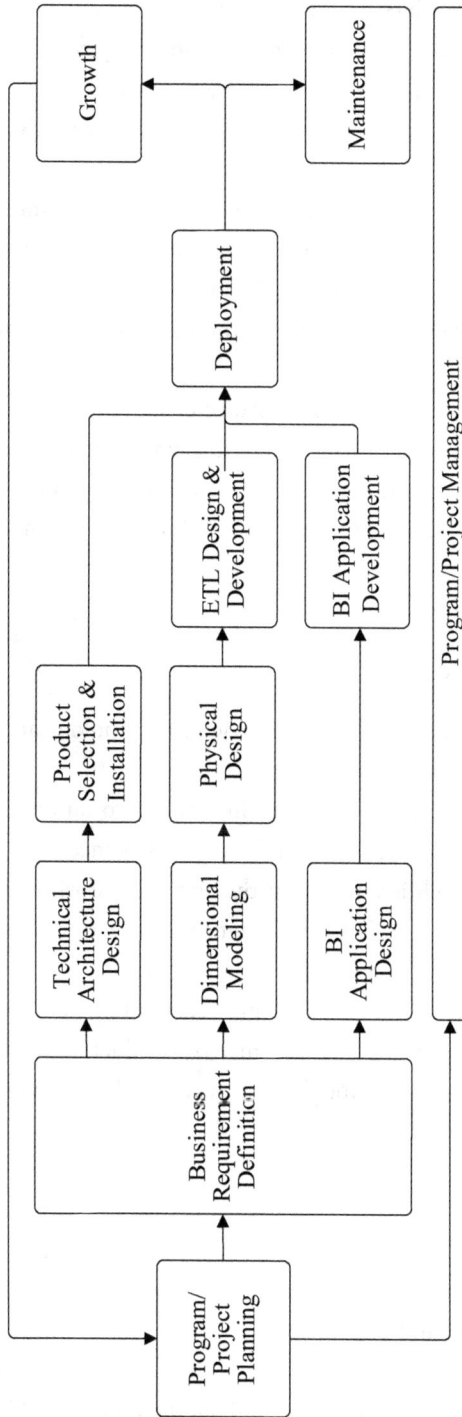

Figure 3.33 The Kimball's life cycle diagram

dimensions are identified, and a list of relevant attributes is created. Ensuring conformity of dimensions (reusable for every facts) enhances consistency and reusability across the data warehouse.

Fact tables are defined based on business events, typically consisting of numerical data that can be aggregated.

Physical design translates the dimensional model into a database schema. It considers technical constraints like software, hardware, and storage capacity. Activities include documenting source systems, setting naming conventions, and optimizing the database for performance and usability.

ETL design and development involve creating processes to populate the data warehouse. This includes building staging tables, implementing data quality checks, defining audit processes, and ensuring security measures are in place. Developers must also optimize the system to efficiently handle large data volumes.

Technology Life Cycle

Kimball emphasizes a structured approach to technology and tools selection and architecture design.

Architecture design involves creating models to outline system components and their interactions. This helps identify inconsistencies, clarify roles and responsibilities, and align the architecture with organizational standards and constraints. A well-designed architecture minimizes technical debt while balancing detail with practicality.

Product selection is required for projects needing new tools. The process includes creating a comparison matrix, conducting market research, validating functionality through prototypes, and finalizing installation through contract negotiation.

BI Application Life Cycle

Kimball's methodology also addresses the life cycle of BI applications, focusing on design and development.

BI applications deliver predefined visualizations and reports, offering quick wins to foster user acceptance and build momentum. Consolidating stakeholder priorities ensures reporting needs are addressed efficiently. Design standards, visualization guidelines, and legal constraints should be considered during this phase.

The development phase creates sustainable solutions. Developers establish naming conventions, formulas, and libraries while adhering to development standards. User training is crucial to ensure proper tool usage and minimize design errors.

The first iteration of a BI application often reveals significant insights, testing the architecture, data models, and data quality while serving as a foundation for further refinement.

Kimball's methodology provides a holistic framework for designing and implementing data warehouses. By addressing both technical and functional needs, it ensures alignment with organizational goals while fostering a robust, scalable solution.

Data Vault

Data Vault is a data modeling methodology designed for scenarios with multiple source systems, frequent changes in relationships, and the need for robust data tracking and auditing. It provides a structure to define tables and relationships before implementing the data warehouse layer.

Unlike Kimball's process-driven modeling approach, which can be volatile due to changes in organizational processes, Data Vault focuses on business concepts that remain relatively stable. Changes in these core concepts indicate a complete business reinvention, making this approach more sustainable over time.

Comparison with Other Models

- 3NF (Third Normal Form): Primarily used in operational systems like ERP (enterprise resource planning) and CRM, optimized for fast access to smaller data sets for both writing and reading.
- Dimensional Modeling (e.g., Kimball): Focused on data warehouses and data marts, optimized for querying large data volumes.
- Data Vault Modeling: Prioritizes integration, historization, and agility, making it suitable for evolving enterprise data warehouses.

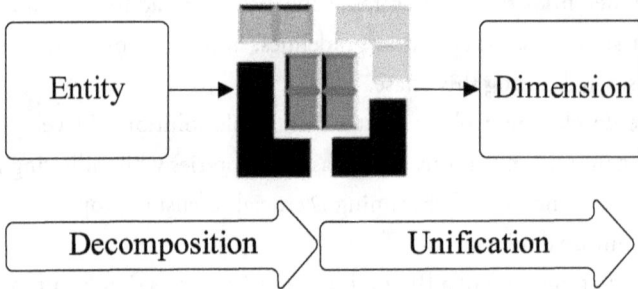

Figure 3.34 Data Vault Entity–Component–Dimension schema

The fundamental principle of Data Vault is *unified decomposition*. This means breaking down business concepts into flexible components while maintaining integration through defined relationships (Figure 3.34).

Core Concepts of Data Vault

Data Vault introduces a unique structure with distinct roles for each model component:

- Hubs: Represent business concepts as natural keys, containing no additional attributes. Examples include sale_id, client_id, or product_code.
- Links: Define relationships between hubs. Each link connects two hubs and contains only relationship attributes. For instance, sale_id/client_id or product_id/category_id.
- Satellites: Hold contextual data, descriptions, and historical records. Satellites share the same primary key as the hub they are associated with, along with a date or timestamp for historization. Satellites can be split to handle data with varying volatilities or sources.

This separation ensures clarity and flexibility in the data model (Figure 3.35).

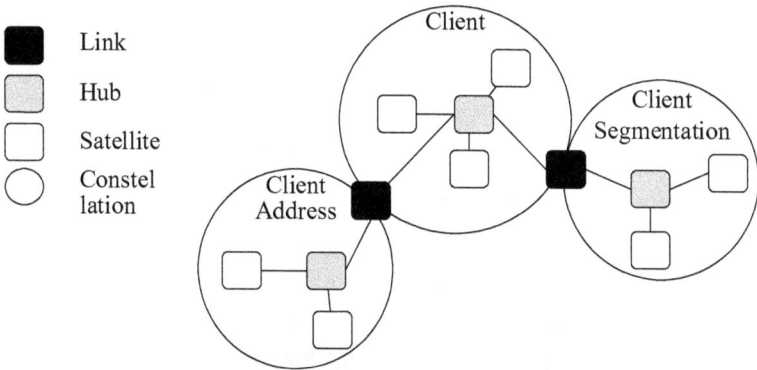

Figure 3.35 Data Vault modelization main concepts

Why and When to Use Data Vault

Advantages:

1. Change Resilience: Ideal for environments with frequent changes to data sources or business processes.
2. Historization and Auditability: Tracks data history and supports audits natively.
3. Incremental Development: Supports agile development by allowing iterative changes.
4. Integration: Facilitates seamless integration and reconciliation of heterogeneous data.
5. Stability: Focus on business concepts rather than processes minimizes disruption from organizational changes.

Challenges:

1. Learning Curve: Technical teams need time and training to adopt the methodology.
2. Increased Complexity: Generates numerous tables and joins, requiring disciplined maintenance and development.
3. Intermediate Layer: Not designed for direct querying by users or reporting tools. Instead, it acts as a foundation for dimensional models and data marts.

Use Cases for Data Vault

When to Enhance Kimball with Data Vault:

- Organizations with multiple, frequently changing data sources
- Enterprises prioritizing historization, traceability, and auditability
- Situations where a siloed approach is no longer viable, and sustainability is essential
- Environments with dynamic business rules or an MDM (Master Data Management) implementation on the roadmap

When to Use Only the Kimball Method:

- Source systems are stable and homogeneous (e.g., a single ERP system).
- The scope is well defined, with limited need for frequent updates or historization.
- Traceability and audits are not a priority (e.g., Sarbanes–Oxley compliance is not required).
- Quick wins and low-cost solutions are the primary objectives.

By balancing its advantages and limitations, Data Vault offers a robust approach for building sustainable and scalable data warehouses in complex and evolving business landscapes.

Limitations

The requirement-gathering process is inherently complex, with no guaranteed checklist to ensure success. While previous chapters have outlined various techniques and methodologies, achieving accurate and comprehensive requirements remains a nuanced task. The diversity of approaches reflects the creative and intellectually enriching nature of this activity, but it also demands navigating numerous challenges to align all stakeholders on the solution to be delivered. This chapter explores the primary factors that limit the scope and precision of requirement gathering.

Social Limitations

The success of requirement gathering heavily depends on the training and engagement of stakeholders and analysts. The analyst must be motivated and trained, understanding the need to balance attention to detail with a realistic approach to precision. Stakeholders, on the other hand, must appreciate the value of requirement gathering to contribute effectively.

Two extremes can hinder the process. On the one hand, excessive trust in the project team's ability to step into the users' shoes can lead to a tunnel vision effect, creating blind spots in understanding. On the other hand, overinvolvement of functional stakeholders, such as producing overly detailed technical requirements, can stifle the technical team's creativity and limit their ability to propose optimal solutions.

Another challenge arises when technical teams are inadequately trained on new platforms, leading to errors in architecture, development, and data quality. Such issues can jeopardize the entire solution and, in some cases, necessitate a complete rebuild.

Beyond training, other social factors can impair the process. Stakeholders' availability, elicitation, and abstraction skills, along with their cultural and experiential diversity, play significant roles. For instance, junior team members may hesitate to challenge senior managers, even on technical matters. Group dynamics and organizational hierarchy can further complicate collaboration. In cultures where contradicting superiors is taboo, achieving meaningful and collaborative discussions may be nearly impossible.

Technical and Functional Limitations

In fast-paced environments with constrained budgets and timelines, requirement gathering is often deprioritized or skipped altogether. This tendency is exacerbated in high-stakes projects where stakeholders demand visible solution progress to feel reassured. Unfortunately, this perception of requirement gathering as unproductive can lead to significant downstream inefficiencies.

Frequent changes in technical and functional domains can also pose challenges. Missing information, such as upcoming legal or regulatory requirements, can make documentation difficult. The granularity of requirements often varies depending on the perspective. While functional stakeholders might prefer high-level descriptions, developers require detailed specifications. The analyst's task is to strike a balance between oversimplified notes and exhaustive documentation.

The context and stakes of a project also influence the required level of precision. For example, a sales forecast may not demand the same rigor as a legal report for a nuclear facility. Similarly, existing solutions and technical platforms may necessitate adjustments in the process. If a current solution already meets most needs or the new solution is temporary, investing in exhaustive documentation or strict adherence to standards may not be justified.

Data limitations often emerge as significant constraints. Missing, insufficient, or unavailable data can render certain requirements impossible to fulfill. Identifying these constraints early can prevent wasted effort on unachievable goals.

Finally, communication skills and language barriers can hinder the process, especially in international contexts. Misunderstandings, ambiguities, and nuances—if not addressed effectively—can compromise the clarity and completeness of captured requirements.

Navigating Limitations

The analyst must navigate these multifaceted limitations to find an optimal approach for the specific project context. While achieving a perfect setup is unrealistic, adapting methods to the situation and understanding their trade-offs can help mitigate risks. By identifying and addressing potential challenges, the analyst can improve the likelihood of delivering a solution that meets stakeholders' needs.

Conclusion

This part has provided a detailed exploration of diverse requirement-gathering techniques, highlighting their application, benefits, and challenges. From the simplicity of interviews and brainstorming sessions to the rigor of systemic thinking and advanced modeling languages, this section underscores the importance of a versatile and context-sensitive approach to requirement elicitation.

A recurring theme is the need for collaboration and clear communication between stakeholders and technical teams. The techniques discussed, such as the Brown Cow model or syntax and grammar analysis, are not just about capturing requirements but also about fostering alignment, reducing ambiguities, and ensuring shared understanding across all levels of the organization.

Moreover, the inclusion of advanced frameworks like Data Vault and EKD demonstrates how structured methodologies can support scalability, agility, and traceability, even in complex projects. These tools help organizations future-proof their solutions while ensuring they remain adaptable to evolving needs.

As readers move forward, they are encouraged to view requirement gathering not as a rigid process but as an opportunity for creativity, discovery, and continuous improvement. By applying the insights and techniques from this part, analysts and stakeholders can confidently navigate the complexities of BI projects, delivering solutions that are not only functional but also aligned with strategic objectives.

CHAPTER 4

Running BI Portfolio Beyond Business Analysis

Requirements and Project Management

BI projects are commonly managed using one of two project management frameworks. The traditional approach, known as "waterfall," is supported by established organizations like the PMI with its PMP (Project Management Professional) certification and PRINCE2 (Projects in Controlled Environments). However, in recent years, these methods have faced competition from agile methodologies, including Scrum and Kanban, which offer greater flexibility and responsiveness.

This chapter examines how requirement gathering intersects with project management, exploring the strengths and limitations of different approaches.

In a Traditional Context

Traditional project management methodologies, such as PMP and PRINCE2, are well suited for creating robust and mature BI solutions. Originally conceptualized by H. D. Bennington in 1956 during the Symposium on Advanced Programming Methods for Digital Computers, the waterfall method was formally named in 1976. While effective in delivering consistent outcomes, it is often criticized for being rigid and less adaptable.

Traditional methods are process-oriented, following a sequential progression of activities. Each phase is defined by specific deliverables with predetermined formats. Despite variations in implementation, these approaches share common goals: gathering requirements, defining the project scope, breaking down tasks, ensuring functional coverage, and managing scope changes effectively (Figure 4.1).

| Elicitate needs | → | Define scope | → | Create WBS | → | Verify scope | → | Control scope |

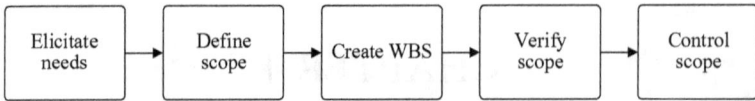

Figure 4.1 Traditional project management process

Requirement Elicitation

Once the project's objectives are established and stakeholders identified, the next step is to document functional stakeholder requirements. Analysts utilize various techniques outlined in Chapter 3. This process typically produces three main deliverables: requirement documentation, a requirement management plan, and a traceability matrix.

Requirement Documentation

Requirement documentation describes the list of needs addressing the project's functional challenges. This document evolves iteratively, transitioning from high-level descriptions to refined details. Each requirement must meet acceptance criteria—nonambiguity, uniqueness, and completeness. The format may vary, including lists, goal trees, or process descriptions. Key components of requirement documentation generally include:

- Project objectives
- Functional and nonfunctional requirements (e.g., security, performance, accessibility)
- Business processes to monitor
- Mock-ups
- Acceptance criteria for solution quality
- Training and implementation needs
- Prerequisites and constraints

Requirement Management Plan

A requirement management plan outlines how project scope will be managed. Although rarely formalized, this document provides clear guidance on validating or rejecting changes and assessing their impacts. Proactively addressing questions such as prioritization methods or defining minor changes ensures smoother project execution.

Traceability Matrix

A traceability matrix links each requirement to project objectives, facilitating justification, impact analysis, and verification. Analysts document project objectives, subobjectives, requirements, stakeholders, priorities, and versions. This ensures alignment between the project's goals and its execution (Figure 4.2).

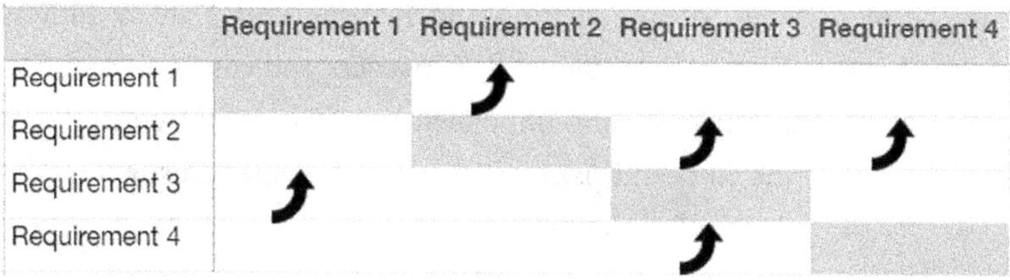

	Requirement 1	Requirement 2	Requirement 3	Requirement 4
Requirement 1		➥		
Requirement 2			➥	➥
Requirement 3	➥			
Requirement 4			➥	

Figure 4.2 Traceability matrix example

Scope Definition

Following requirement elicitation, scope definition establishes project boundaries. This step involves consulting domain experts or conducting product analyses to identify tasks, estimate costs, and evaluate feasibility. By prioritizing requirements and constraints, the team defines what falls within or outside the project scope. Alternative analyses can identify optimal implementation options.

Work Breakdown Structure

The work breakdown structure (WBS) outlines all activities required to deliver the solution. Starting from the final deliverable (e.g., a report or table), components are broken into tasks. Reusability of components is emphasized to avoid redundant work. WBS documentation includes task descriptions, responsibilities, timelines, costs, quality expectations, and technical references.

Scope Verification

Scope verification, often referred to as testing in IT, ensures deliverables meet defined requirements. This process aligns the solution design with organizational goals and stakeholder expectations. Workshops involving stakeholders are particularly valuable for validating reports and data models. Early verification prevents tunnel effects, where misaligned deliverables create project inefficiencies.

Change Management

Change management in traditional project management involves updating the requirement documentation and management plan to address scope changes. Tools such as traceability matrices and continuity models are invaluable for analyzing and implementing changes efficiently. These tools minimize the costs and risks associated with scope adjustments.

Advantages of the Waterfall Approach

The waterfall method offers numerous benefits:

1. Process Orientation: These methods rely on well-defined processes, reducing the dependency on individual expertise and facilitating structured workflows.
2. High-Quality Outputs: The focus on rigorous processes ensures robust and reliable deliverables.
3. Comprehensive Approach: Designed for complex and critical projects, traditional methods excel in managing dependencies and delivering consistent results.
4. Change Management: Formalized change processes prevent unnecessary adjustments driven by individual agendas.
5. Knowledge Sustainability: Extensive documentation supports long-term knowledge retention, especially in organizations with high staff turnover.
6. Budget and Scope Control: Fixed budgets and scopes provide clear boundaries, with changes subject to approval and budgetary extensions.

Limitations of the Waterfall Approach

Despite its strengths, the waterfall approach has drawbacks:

1. Rigidity: The method's inflexibility can lead to excessive focus on processes rather than the product's value.
2. Inefficiency for Small Projects: For smaller projects, comprehensive documentation may be unnecessary and demotivating and an overkill.
3. Formal Communication: Limited interaction between functional and technical stakeholders can hinder efficiency and innovation. It also produces a "tunnel effect."

In an Agile Context

Agile methodologies have gained significant traction as an alternative to traditional project management approaches. Focused on lean management principles, Agile aims to deliver high-quality products efficiently by emphasizing adaptability, prioritization, and collaboration over rigid processes and comprehensive documentation.

The Agile Process

The cornerstone of Agile lies in its roots in lean management, a concept originating from the Toyota Production System in the 1990s. This approach emphasizes eliminating inefficiencies, known as the "seven wastes," which include overproduction, excess inventory, unnecessary motion, defects, overprocessing, waiting time, and redundant transport. These principles are seamlessly applicable to BI, addressing common inefficiencies such as excessive data redundancy, overcomplex processes, untrained teams, and misaligned resources.

Agile methodologies prioritize delivering high-value features to stakeholders by eliminating components with minimal or no added value. This is achieved through adaptability and responsiveness rather than strict adherence to predefined plans.

The Agile Manifesto outlines core principles that guide this methodology:

- Individuals and interactions over processes and tools
- Working solutions over extensive documentation
- Customer collaboration over contract negotiation
- Responding to change over following a plan (Figure 4.3)

Agile places people at the center of its approach, fostering close collaboration between stakeholders and technical teams to align requirements with delivered solutions.

Differences from Traditional Approaches

While the initial requirement elicitation phase remains similar to traditional methods, Agile distinguishes itself by integrating development and requirement gathering. Functional and technical stakeholders, along with development teams, collaborate closely to create user stories and mock-ups, minimizing the need for detailed technical specifications. Prioritization is key, focusing on high-impact deliverables while limiting interdependencies.

Unlike traditional methods, Agile promotes iterative scope negotiation. This continuous process defines what will be delivered in each

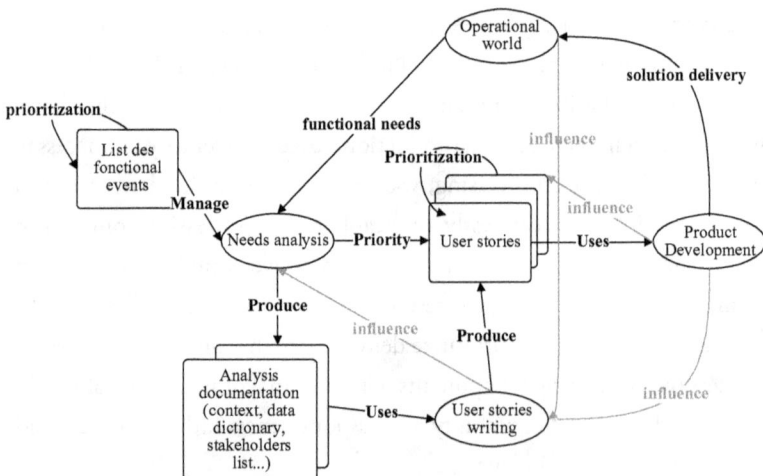

Figure 4.3 Agile requirement management process

iteration, ranging from short sprints (two weeks) to longer cycles (up to two months).

The Agile Requirement Process

Agile's requirement management emphasizes business over technical needs. Acknowledging the inevitability of change, Agile opts for light documentation and iterative development. Teams often proceed with development even as requirements are being refined, fostering parallel collaboration among multidisciplinary team members.

Process Flow

The typical process flow of Agile is:

1. Triggering Events: Business needs arise from triggering events such as decisions, process changes, or external factors.
2. Requirement Analysis: Analysts identify stakeholders, prioritize triggers, and generate artifacts like scenarios or business cases.
3. Feature Definition: Using artifacts, teams collaboratively define technical and functional requirements, ensuring user-centric solutions.
4. User Stories: Developed collaboratively, user stories articulate business needs and are prioritized in the development backlog.
5. Development and Validation: The team iteratively refines and develops the solution, aligning with business priorities and technical feasibility.

Writing Effective User Stories

User stories should:

- Focus on outcomes, driven by triggering events.
- Maintain a balanced granularity, falling between product use cases and atomic requirements.
- Align with business goals and technical requirements.
- Use consistent formats, such as:

"As [Role], I need [Functionality], because/when/in order to [Triggering Event]."

Tools like the Volere framework support the definition and refinement of user stories, ensuring alignment with organizational goals.

Key Roles in Agile Methodologies

1. Product Owner: Representing users and stakeholders, the Product Owner defines and prioritizes functional requirements. This role demands domain expertise, technical knowledge, and decision-making authority to guide the team effectively.
2. Technical Team: Comprising developers, architects, and technical specialists, the team collaborates closely and operates with autonomy. Members must be versatile, communicative, and skilled in cross-functional roles, exemplifying the "T-shaped" professional model.
3. Analyst: The analyst facilitates discussions, oversees requirements elicitation, and ensures a balanced perspective between functional and technical aspects. They play a pivotal role in aligning the solution with business needs.
4. Management: Agile management fosters collaboration, supports prioritization, and resolves conflicts. Managers ensure alignment between Agile teams and organizational goals, facilitating knowledge sharing and team synchronization.

Advantages of Agile Methodologies

Agile methodologies offer significant flexibility, allowing projects to adapt to evolving requirements and changes in the business environment. This adaptability ensures that deliverables align closely with current needs and priorities, enabling rapid value delivery to stakeholders. One of Agile's key strengths is its iterative approach, which emphasizes delivering the most critical components first. This prioritization means stakeholders can begin using and benefiting from the solution early in the project life cycle, while also providing valuable feedback for subsequent iterations.

Agile's people-centered focus encourages close collaboration among team members and stakeholders. This collaboration fosters creativity, improves communication, and allows teams to identify and address challenges promptly. By testing and learning during development, Agile minimizes the risks of costly rework and ensures that the solution remains aligned with user expectations. Additionally, Agile's iterative nature can simplify adaptation to technical changes, such as platform upgrades or new tools, by integrating these updates incrementally without significant disruption.

Limitations of Agile Methodologies

Despite its many advantages, Agile methodologies come with limitations. The iterative and reactive nature of Agile often focuses on short-term goals and well-defined needs, making it less suitable for projects with complex, long-term requirements or dependencies. As team size increases, communication becomes more challenging, and the risk of misalignment among stakeholders rises. Larger projects also face difficulties in knowledge management due to Agile's lighter emphasis on documentation, potentially leading to gaps in understanding over time.

A significant challenge in Agile is balancing the immediate needs of stakeholders with the broader objectives of the organization. Stakeholders may prioritize quick results, whereas the organization might benefit more from scalable and reusable solutions. This divergence can lead to conflicts and suboptimal solutions that fail to address long-term goals.

Team composition is another critical factor. Agile relies heavily on skilled, self-motivated, and collaborative team members. Finding individuals with the necessary expertise and interpersonal skills can be difficult, and conflicts or unclear scopes can further complicate teamwork.

Finally, Agile methodologies can struggle with managing complex dependencies inherent in BI projects, where components like data models and reporting tools are tightly interlinked. The constant adjustments and rework required in Agile can lead to inefficiencies and increased costs, particularly when requirements are not well defined or change frequently. This lack of predictability also complicates budgeting and cost management, making Agile less suited for projects with fixed contracts or strict deadlines (Figure 4.4).

Figure 4.4 Infinite monkey theorem by **The Simpsons**

Scaling Agile

Agile methodologies are inherently suited to small-to-medium projects with independent needs. Scaling Agile to larger, more complex projects requires segmenting platforms into modular components with clear interfaces. As Agile practices mature, strategies for managing dependencies and knowledge across long-term projects need to be addressed.

When to Use Agile

Agile methodologies are best suited for projects with independent tasks and relatively simple requirements, where flexibility and adaptability are prioritized. They are particularly effective for visualization-focused deliverables, such as creating dashboards or reports, where requirements can evolve and feedback is essential. Agile is also beneficial for organizations that value iterative development, enabling teams to deliver incremental value and adjust priorities based on ongoing insights and stakeholder input.

However, Agile is less ideal for projects involving critical applications or those requiring long-term stability, such as legal reporting or strategic architecture projects. It is also less effective for complex and interdependent BI projects, where strong dependencies between components demand a more structured approach. Additionally, Agile methodologies may not align well with fixed budgets and rigid contractual obligations, where scope and costs need to be clearly defined from the outset. For these scenarios, a traditional or hybrid approach might be more appropriate.

Evaluate the BI Maturity

Understanding the Importance of BI Maturity Evaluation

Evaluating the maturity of your BI ecosystem is essential for several reasons. It provides a clear understanding of the value currently delivered by the BI infrastructure and identifies areas that require improvement. This evaluation serves as a baseline for crafting a strategic roadmap, enabling organizations to prioritize changes and enhance their BI capabilities systematically.

Incorporating maturity evaluation into the requirements-gathering process is particularly beneficial. It helps uncover bottlenecks and facilitates collaboration across departments. By offering stakeholders a comprehensive overview of the current BI status, it enables them to identify shared pain points and agree on priority areas to address. This alignment ensures that efforts are focused on achieving organizational objectives more effectively.

Moreover, assessing BI maturity fosters a sense of shared purpose among management and teams. It highlights common challenges and opportunities, both within the company and across industries. When communicated as part of a BI roadmap, maturity evaluation generates enthusiasm and eases the cultural, organizational, and technical transitions required to advance BI initiatives.

Dimensions of BI Maturity Models

Various BI maturity models exist in the literature, with each emphasizing specific facets of BI ecosystems. No single model comprehensively covers all aspects, but they collectively offer valuable frameworks. According to Lahrmann et al., in *Business Intelligence Maturity: An Overview* (2010), BI maturity is typically assessed across multiple dimensions, including:

- Application: The types of analytical tools in use, such as reporting, OLAP, or data mining
- Architecture: The structure of source systems, platforms, and integration infrastructure
- Behavior: The decision-making culture within the organization, emphasizing fact-based approaches
- Change: The extent to which changes are controlled and tracked over time
- Data: The breadth of subject areas, data models, and the quality and quantity of data
- Efficiency: The ratio of resource input to output
- Impact: Both individual and organizational outcomes influenced by BI
- Infrastructure: Components of the integration framework, including databases and application servers
- Organizational Structure: The placement and structure of the BI function within the organization
- Processes: The maturity of BI-related processes and activities
- Staff: The skills, experience, and specialization of BI personnel
- Strategy: The alignment of BI with corporate, business, and IT objectives
- Users: The type, number, and geographical distribution of BI users (Figure 4.5)

BI Maturity Models

This chapter focuses on two widely recognized BI maturity models:

1. TDWI (The Data Warehousing Institute) BI Maturity Model
   This foundational model has been widely adopted and adapted as a base for subsequent maturity frameworks. It offers a detailed structure for evaluating and improving BI maturity.

Dimension	TDWI	SAS	Eckerson	SMC	Cates & Assoc.	Dataflux	Sen & Assoc.	HP	Gartner	Teradata
Application	yes		yes	yes				yes	yes	yes
Architecture	yes		yes				yes			
Behavior		yes	yes				yes		yes	
Change	yes	yes					yes			
Data	yes				yes	yes	yes		yes	yes
Efficiency	yes									
Impact	yes		yes			yes		yes	yes	yes
Infrastructure		yes	yes	yes		yes	yes	yes	yes	
Org. structure				yes				yes	yes	
Processes		yes		yes		yes				
Staff	yes									
Strategy								yes		
Users	yes	yes	yes	yes	yes	yes				

Figure 4.5 Maturity model comparative table

2. Gartner BI Maturity Model

Developed by the Gartner Group, a leading authority in industry standards, this model is frequently used due to its comprehensive and practical approach. It reflects best practices and widely accepted benchmarks, making it an invaluable tool for organizations.

For further insights, the following figure summarizes the dimensions covered by different BI maturity models, as described by Lahrmann et al. Selecting the most suitable model depends on the specific context and objectives of your organization.

TDWI Business Intelligence Maturity Model

TDWI Business Intelligence Maturity Model, developed by Wayne Eckerson in 2004 (cited in Lahmann et al. 2010), provides a framework for evaluating the evolution of BI ecosystems across eight dimensions: Application, Architecture, Change, Data, Efficiency, Impact, Staff, and Users. These dimensions are grouped under broader categories such as Scope, Sponsorship, Funding Value, Architecture, Data, Development, and Delivery. The model emphasizes technical maturity and categorizes BI ecosystems into six progressive stages: Prenatal, Infant, Child, Teenager, Adult, and Sage.

Prenatal Stage

The prenatal phase represents the pre-data-warehouse stage, where reporting is limited to operational systems. Reports are generated using spreadsheets or directly from operational applications, often involving labor-intensive processes. Multisource reporting is cumbersome and lacks agility, requiring users to manually reconcile data sources and define governance elements such as KPIs. This decentralized approach leads to inefficiencies, as users must create their own reports and workaround solutions.

Infant Stage

The infant stage builds on the prenatal phase and is often characterized by early attempts at data organization. Business stakeholders primarily rely on static operational reports, still heavily dependent on spreadsheets and desktop databases, commonly known as spreadmarts. At this stage, there is minimal correlation between data, metrics, and rules, resulting in conflicting and fragmented insights. The BI system struggles to support cohesive business objectives or decision-making processes.

Child Stage

In the child stage, organizations begin to establish more structured BI practices. Skilled employees join the BI community, and interactive reporting tools are introduced. Regional data warehouses are developed, catering to specific business units or a limited group of users. These warehouses primarily pull data from operational systems, often without ensuring cross-dataset or cross-unit compatibility. While trends and historical data become more accessible, limitations in data quality, poor planning, and cultural resistance to decommissioning spreadmarts hinder progress.

Teenager Stage

At the teenager stage, the organization adopts standardized methodologies and best practices. External consultants may be brought in to assist with creating a unified data model and platform. Stakeholders begin to recognize the value of consolidated reporting and models. Enterprise-wide analyses enable deeper insights, dashboards are tailored for specific user groups, and KPIs are formally defined. Key users and stakeholders actively engage with dashboards and other analytical tools, reflecting growing BI maturity.

Adult Stage

Organizations at the adult stage shift from tactical to strategic BI practices. Central IT systems drive operations, and dashboards monitor data processes in real time. BI capabilities extend to predictive analytics, performance management, and centralized reporting, allowing executive management to make informed decisions. Data sources are centrally managed, and the architecture is layered, ensuring flexibility and reducing the impact of changes on the system. Real-time integration of diverse data sources enhances the accuracy and depth of analyses. However, bridging gaps between regional data warehouses to achieve a unified source of truth remains a challenge. Strong executive support is essential to reach and sustain this level of maturity.

Sage Stage

The sage stage represents the pinnacle of BI maturity, where organizations integrate BI into both technical and business services, often managed through a center of excellence (COE). Development processes are distributed, and reports are fully customizable. A centralized information management group oversees a comprehensive data repository, supported by a service-oriented architecture (SOA). At this level, the system incorporates distributed development, robust data services, and extended enterprise capabilities, including partnerships with suppliers, clients, and other stakeholders. Developers are well trained and certified, and alignment between business and IT fosters greater collaboration. This stage is marked by a diverse and expanding user base, along with a highly optimized and scalable BI infrastructure.

The Gartner Maturity Model for Business Intelligence and Performance Management

Gartner's Maturity Model for Business Intelligence and Performance Management provides a framework for assessing the maturity of an organization or a single business unit's BI practices. The model categorizes maturity into five levels: Unaware, Tactical, Focused, Strategic, and Pervasive, while evaluating three key areas: People, Processes, and Metrics and Technology.

Unaware

This stage, often referred to as "information anarchy," reflects an organization with minimal understanding or use of BI.

- People: BI users lack awareness of data's value and its role in decision making.
- Processes: Efforts are focused on meeting isolated departmental needs. Information management is typically seen as IT's responsibility, funded through an IT budget and tied to a single cost center.
- Metrics and Technology: Performance management KPIs are poorly defined, with inconsistent and inaccurate data interpretations. Reporting is primarily spreadsheet-based, occasionally supplemented by basic reporting tools.

Tactical

At the tactical level, organizations begin recognizing the need for BI but lack a cohesive approach.

- People: Users lack the necessary training and skills to fully utilize the BI platform. Management raises concerns about report quality and consistency.
- Processes: Initial BI investments emerge, often spearheaded by IT. However, limited management support leads to underfunded initiatives.
- Metrics and Technology: Metrics are typically defined at the departmental level, with little to no alignment across the organization. Data and reporting remain siloed, using either spreadsheets or off-the-shelf tools.

Focused

This level marks the establishment of foundational BI practices within specific organizational areas.

- People: Users receive basic training, enabling them to conduct simple analyses. BI competency centers emerge, fostering collaboration between business and IT professionals to address stakeholder needs.

- Processes: Early successes demonstrate the value of BI, though its scope remains confined to certain departments. A senior departmental leader or IT sponsor often drives the initiative, with funding coming from one or more business units.
- Metrics and Technology: Metrics are inconsistently defined and sourced, even at the departmental level. Data integration remains limited, and available tools only address a portion of business requirements.

Strategic

At this stage, BI becomes a core part of the organization's strategy, driving more significant value.

- People: Trained users can make tactical and strategic decisions using data. BI capabilities extend to suppliers, partners, and sometimes customers.
- Processes: BI and performance management are recognized as critical business processes, supported by executive-level sponsorship. The BI competency center receives sufficient funding to align with organizational goals.
- Metrics and Technology: Data and metrics are trusted across all levels of the organization. BI informs financial and strategic objectives, with a robust framework for data quality, governance, and management in place.

Pervasive

This represents the highest level of BI maturity, where BI is deeply embedded into organizational culture.

- People: Users are skilled in complex analysis and actively support data quality and policy management. They access all necessary information to enhance business performance and outcomes.

- Processes: BI is perceived as a critical business process and integral to decision-making culture. The BI competency center is proactive, adapting to changes and meeting evolving business needs. BI's measurable benefits are closely tied to organizational goals.
- Metrics and Technology: Metrics and information are universally trusted, aligning stakeholders across the organization, suppliers, partners, and customers. Misinterpretations of data are minimal, facilitating seamless communication and collaboration.

Final Thoughts

Organizations at lower maturity levels require substantial resources to establish a solid foundation for BI practices. As they progress, the true potential of analytics becomes apparent, driving transformation and alignment with business goals. The following chapter provides a step-by-step guide to crafting a successful BI strategy that enables effective insights and fosters organizational growth.

Create a BI Strategy Step-by-Step

Importance of a BI Strategy

The primary goal of a BI strategy is to align actions and resources with the organization's overarching objectives. According to the 2020 Global State of Enterprise Analytics survey, 45 percent of businesses prioritize analytics efforts to develop new business models and eliminate inefficiencies in data access. This highlights how integral data is to achieving organizational goals and addressing challenges.

Planning the BI and analytics capability is crucial for supporting the company's strategy. Tools, teams, training, and focal areas must be aligned, while business processes need to operate cohesively to deliver quality results. A well-defined BI strategy also justifies investments, as it helps direct resources toward initiatives that yield the most significant value and measurable outcomes.

A robust data strategy drives improvements in several key areas:

- Unified Source of Truth: Establishing a single, consistent version of the truth across the organization facilitates stakeholder collaboration and minimizes wasted time caused by conflicting information or misinterpretations.
- Consistent Definitions: Uniform definitions of metrics and dimensions enhance the reuse of technical components, simplify reporting consolidation, and improve communication among diverse stakeholders.
- Optimized BI Resource Management: BI specialists and analysts are empowered to maintain a cohesive ecosystem, preventing disparate departments from creating isolated, redundant solutions. This alignment ensures BI assets contribute effectively to organizational goals.
- Enhanced Data Quality: Prioritizing data quality mitigates the risk of making decisions based on inaccurate or incomplete data, ensuring a reliable foundation for critical decisions.

Not every organization will need to follow the same sequence of steps in crafting a BI strategy, as the process should be adapted to the organization's unique context and needs.

Securing an Executive Sponsor

The executive sponsor plays a pivotal role in driving the BI initiative forward while maintaining a long-term vision. Their primary responsibilities include promoting the BI initiative, ensuring alignment with organizational goals, and fostering stability in pursuit of long-term objectives over short-term gains.

As a key figure, the sponsor works to secure buy-in from other C-level executives and stakeholders, effectively demonstrating the value and potential of BI for the organization. They help maintain alignment between the organization's strategic goals and the BI initiative, ensuring that the project delivers meaningful impact.

Ideally, the sponsor is a leader with the authority to influence policies and procedures across the organization. Their role extends to leading and coordinating change management efforts between various business units, ensuring smooth transitions and effective collaboration.

The sponsor must possess the authority to allocate resources, such as funding and personnel time, to the initiative. Their influence is instrumental in securing project budgets and ensuring that BI portfolios receive the necessary support. This authority also empowers them to address obstacles and keep the project on track.

Finally, the sponsor should be someone respected by the CIO, CTO, and other senior leaders, enabling them to organize and steer company-wide initiatives effectively. By gaining not only approval but also active support from stakeholders, the sponsor ensures the initiative's success and long-term sustainability.

Defining Business Objectives

Once a sponsor has been assigned, the primary business objectives must be established. These objectives are critical as they provide a foundation for the initiative, offering stakeholders a clear vision and aligning the scope and priorities for everyone involved.

The sponsor will prioritize the organization's business goals, setting KPIs for each objective to define what success looks like. This process involves consolidating and synthesizing the needs of various business units to ensure alignment with the BI framework. By doing so, the sponsor fosters commitment and excitement among stakeholders while building momentum and trust across both business and technical teams.

Visibility into the value that BI can deliver is crucial for ensuring the initiative's long-term sustainability. Clear objectives help allocate resources effectively, making it easier to measure outcomes and assess the overall benefits of BI. These well-defined goals also serve as a foundation for demonstrating ROI, which is essential for maintaining stakeholders' confidence.

In most cases, finance and sales are the first business units to be addressed during the initial phase of a BI initiative. These areas often provide straightforward opportunities for measuring ROI, and their business and technical requirements are typically well established. A cost/opportunity analysis can help the sponsor identify and prioritize low-hanging fruits, with early successes proving the value of the initiative.

It is important to avoid limiting the definition of business objectives to only the immediate scope of the project. Long-term goals should also be considered, as they influence technical decisions, particularly regarding platform choices. For example, a platform designed solely for monitoring and measuring will differ significantly from one built for advanced analytics, including predictive and prescriptive capabilities. Defining objectives minimizes the risk of ad hoc reporting derailing the project to serve the interests of individual stakeholders rather than creating an organization-wide solution.

Technical and technological goals should be derived from business objectives, as they will determine the tools and skills required for successful implementation. According to the Gartner Group, there are four main types of analytics, each impacting technical requirements differently:

- Descriptive Analytics: Focused on the past, descriptive analytics describes what has happened and is currently happening by providing accurate facts. Common tools include scheduled reports, OLAP, data discovery, and ad hoc reporting, alongside activities like data/text mining, drill-downs, and drill-across analyses.
- Diagnostic Analytics: Slightly more advanced than descriptive analytics, diagnostic analytics aims to uncover why certain events occurred through root cause analysis. Tools include visualization, network/cluster analysis, alerting, and semantic and sentiment analysis.
- Predictive Analytics: Concentrating on the future, predictive analytics anticipates potential outcomes based on historical data. It highlights various scenarios, projects forecasts, and simulates possibilities while accounting for uncertainties. Tools commonly used include predictive modeling, pattern matching,

multivariate statistics, regression analysis, machine learning, and forecasting.

- Prescriptive Analytics: This advanced form of analytics determines the best course of action to achieve or influence desired outcomes. Complementing predictive analytics, it answers the question: "What actions can we take now to improve predictions?" Tools include simulation (Monte Carlo), neural networks, graph analytics, heuristics/rule engines, complex-event processing (CEP), and operations research techniques like optimization (Figure 4.6).

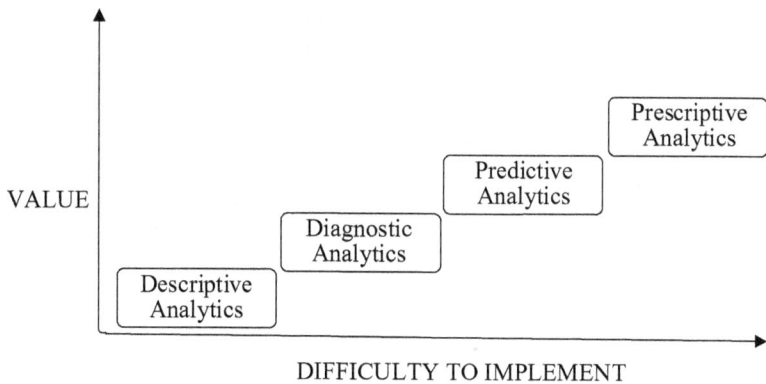

DIFFICULTY TO IMPLEMENT

Figure 4.6 Core analytics techniques by value and complexity

By addressing these analytics types, organizations can ensure their BI strategy aligns with business objectives, supports key decisions, and drives sustained value across all levels of the organization.

Identifying the Key Stakeholders

Identifying the key stakeholders and ensuring the right individuals are involved in discussions is critical to the success of a BI initiative. Stakeholders are traditionally categorized using a matrix based on their level of interest and power in relation to the project (Figure 4.7).

- Promoters/Drivers: These stakeholders hold both high power and high interest in the project. The sponsor is typically the primary

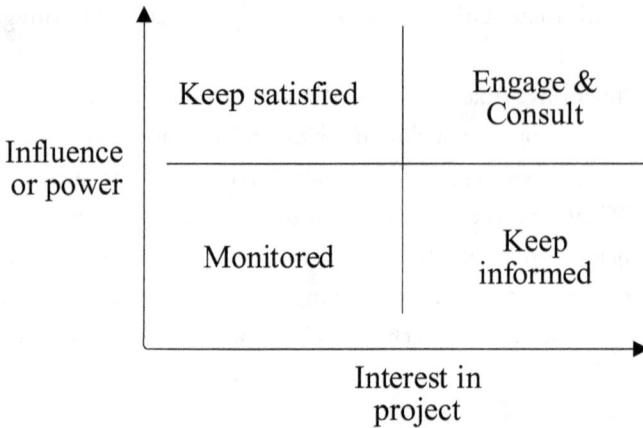

Figure 4.7 Stakeholders matrix

promoter. They are essential players and must be closely engaged
throughout the project.

- Defenders/Supporters: With high interest but low power, these
  stakeholders should be kept informed, and their concerns must be
  considered to ensure their continued support.
- Latents/Bystanders: These individuals have high power but low
  interest. The project team should focus on satisfying their needs
  to prevent potential disruptions.
- Apathetics/Blockers: These stakeholders have low power and low
  interest. Minimal effort should be directed toward them unless
  their involvement becomes critical.

The main business stakeholders, including C-level executives and department heads, play a pivotal role in strategic discussions. Collaborating
with the BI sponsor, they articulate the needs of their teams and help
negotiate project priorities. This group ensures the initiative aligns with
the organization's long-term vision and mitigates the risks of frequent
priority shifts. Furthermore, they establish how BI will be embedded into
organizational processes and outline its potential impact.

It is equally important to identify technical stakeholders. This group
encompasses the BI team, machine learning developers, and supporting
teams such as administrators, network engineers, and storage specialists. These technical contributors ensure the project's infrastructure and

development align with the defined business objectives, providing the foundation for a robust and sustainable BI ecosystem.

Choosing a Platform

Selecting the right platform hinges on the organization's long-term goals and whether the focus is on descriptive, diagnostic, predictive, or prescriptive analytics. The decision-making process involves collaboration between the technical team, the sponsor, and technical stakeholders to ensure the chosen solution aligns with the organization's medium- and long-term objectives.

Assessing Existing Assets

Evaluating the organization's current assets is essential to determine how well they contribute to business objectives. The technical team should identify what works, what doesn't, and what is missing to achieve the long-term goals. This evaluation should focus on four primary aspects: data collection and management, storage, data visualization tools and dashboards, and data governance and access.

- Data Collection and Management: It is critical to understand the business processes and data required to support organizational objectives. Key questions include: What sources are needed, and are they internal or external? Can the volume and historical data requirements be anticipated? Who will manage and prepare the data? What standards and legal constraints are in place for data handling?
- Storage: Deciding between on-premise storage and cloud solutions depends on anticipated data volumes, scalability, and cost-effectiveness. A cost-opportunity analysis can estimate storage requirements, assess ROI by dataset, and forecast migration costs. It is also essential to ensure the storage solution can scale efficiently in the face of uncertainty.
- Data Visualization Tools and Dashboards: Choosing the right visualization and reporting tools involves considering user data

literacy and their reporting needs—whether for simple operational reports or complex analyses. Internal-only solutions offer the advantage of training and support. Balancing flexibility for experienced analysts and developers with ease of use for nontechnical users and management is crucial. Tools range from those optimized for visual analytics and data exploration to those designed for storytelling and explanatory purposes.

- Data Governance and Access: Defining access policies is vital to ensure secure and efficient data use. Questions to address include: What levels of access are needed for different user roles? Who will be allowed to view, modify, or create data? What measures should be implemented to guard against external threats and internal misuse? The governance strategy must align with organizational goals, data-sharing policies, and security guidelines.

Benchmarking and Validation

Once the objectives and current assets are assessed, conducting an industry benchmark is the next step. This can involve creating a custom benchmark tailored to the organization's context, using a benchmark provided by an IT company, or referencing established industry standards like Gartner's Magic Quadrant.

If working with an IT supplier for benchmarking, it is critical to ensure their recommendations are unbiased and not influenced by partnerships with specific tool providers.

Finally, technical feasibility must be validated through prototyping. At this stage, only high-fidelity prototypes should be created to test specific technical elements. These prototypes help confirm whether the proposed solutions meet the required technical specifications.

Defining BI and Technical Roadmaps

Creating two distinct roadmaps—one for BI and the other for technical implementation—is essential to align organizational goals and technical capabilities effectively.

BI Roadmap

The BI roadmap outlines a timeline that highlights objectives, milestones, and actionable steps to support the organization's strategic goals. It can also detail the defined objectives, implementation approaches, resource allocations, and training plans. Typically, the timeline is segmented into phases, with each phase involving specific departments and showcasing the datasets expected to be ready at each stage. This phased approach ensures stakeholder engagement at the right time.

When a platform rollout or migration is required, the roadmap captures these aspects from both technical (infrastructure and components) and functional (user capabilities) perspectives. This dual focus ensures the organization can plan adequately for implementation and training.

For larger-scale projects with many stakeholders, the roadmap may also include a communication plan to maintain alignment and transparency.

Technical Roadmap

The technical roadmap provides a detailed view of the rollout for data storage, BI practices, and associated technologies. It must consider software vendors' upgrade schedules and migration plans, as these can influence the organization's overall technical timeline. Additionally, it should account for broader industry trends to ensure the organization stays competitive and up-to-date with emerging technologies.

Security measures are often a key component of the technical roadmap, defining timelines for implementing safeguards for both internal and external users. The security timeline should align with the availability of datasets and organizational priorities.

Data governance, although frequently overlooked, should also be addressed in the technical roadmap. This includes a timeline for implementing governance policies and identifying key focus areas. A well-defined governance roadmap enables the organization to measure its benefits and successes effectively.

Shared Benefits of Both Roadmaps

Both the BI and technical roadmaps serve as tools to establish ownership and accountability. They help team members articulate their roles while understanding the broader context of the initiative. Additionally, roadmaps provide an opportunity to anticipate potential roadblocks and risks, enabling proactive planning and risk mitigation.

If significant changes are expected, the roadmaps can incorporate a change management plan. They can also align with metrics and individual objectives, such as annual performance goals, ensuring that all teams work cohesively toward common objectives.

An executive summary at the beginning of the roadmap can further enhance its effectiveness. By clearly illustrating the alignment between BI initiatives and corporate strategies, presenting viable alternatives, and defining KPIs, the summary equips sponsors with a powerful tool to communicate and influence stakeholders effectively.

Organizing the BI Team

To effectively implement the roadmap, the organization may need to recruit new talent while retaining and training existing staff. The BI team is traditionally composed of five key roles or functions, which may be labeled differently depending on the organizational context (e.g., agile vs. waterfall methodologies), company structure, or division of responsibilities between teams:

- BI Director: This individual has both business and technical expertise and is responsible for steering the execution of the BI strategy. Their role includes implementing processes, organizing team efforts, and overseeing the roadmaps to ensure alignment with organizational goals.
- BI Engineers: This group is tasked with designing, building, implementing, and maintaining all BI systems. Their responsibilities include managing data, reporting tools, platforms, security measures, networks, servers, and database administration.

- Business Analyst and Quality Analyst: These professionals bridge the gap between business needs and technical execution. They analyze business problems and objectives, translating them into functional or technical requirements that guide development efforts.
- Data Scientist: The data scientist applies analytics, statistics, and machine learning techniques to uncover insights and trends. They develop algorithms and models to predict future outcomes and support data-driven decision making.

Preparing Data Architecture

The final step in the preparation process involves designing a robust architecture to support the BI solution. This begins with evaluating the strengths and weaknesses of the current architecture to understand what works and what needs improvement.

Next, the target architecture is defined—considering both short-term objectives and long-term goals. The ideal architecture should be capable of supporting current requirements while remaining adaptable to future needs.

Once the ideal target architecture is outlined, the organization must assess what can be realistically implemented within the given timeframe. If the target architecture has clear visibility, its development and deployment can be integrated into the roadmap to ensure a structured and phased rollout.

Create BI Governance Step-by-Step

This approach offers a structured framework to address most BI projects effectively. It empowers business analysts to achieve both short time-to-market goals and sustainable, long-term solutions. By adopting this methodology, organizations can ensure alignment between their data initiatives and strategic objectives while delivering high-value insights in a consistent and scalable manner. This chapter highlights the advantages of gaining a high-level understanding of the approach and provides a clear, step-by-step guide to its implementation, illustrated with a consistent example throughout. While this overview offers a structured synthesis of best practices, readers can refer to other chapters for in-depth explanations of each step, as these have already been explored in detail earlier in the book.

Expected Benefits of the Structured Approach

The structured approach provides numerous benefits at both the solution level and the project level, ensuring alignment with organizational goals and promoting sustainable BI initiatives.

Organizational Benefits

Implementing this structured BI governance framework offers a wide range of organizational benefits, beyond project execution and technical consistency. These benefits collectively support stronger alignment, efficiency, and adaptability at all levels of the enterprise:

- Breaking down business and technical silos: By facilitating structured, iterative conversations between business and IT stakeholders, the framework encourages collaboration across departments. This creates shared ownership of definitions, KPIs, processes, and outcomes, and fosters a common language across functions.
- Mutualizing initiatives to minimize costs: Instead of launching redundant or disconnected efforts, BI governance allows teams to identify overlaps and mutualize developments. This leads to significant cost savings by reusing data models, standard KPIs, and reporting components across departments.
- Establishing global structure and oversight: The framework offers a clear structure for aligning BI initiatives with organizational strategy, making it easier for leadership to maintain a high-level overview and exercise strategic control across multiple business units.

- Enhancing cross-functional business alignment: By encouraging shared objectives, standardized concepts, and unified metrics, the framework reinforces alignment between departments. This alignment ensures that efforts converge on common priorities rather than competing agendas.
- Institutionalizing a data-driven culture: The governance process helps embed data literacy and analytical thinking within the organization. As data become central to decision making, teams shift from intuition-based decisions to evidence-based strategies.
- Improving change resilience: With formalized documentation of goals, processes, and data standards, the organization becomes more agile. It can adapt to new technologies, strategic pivots, or personnel changes without losing coherence or retracing previous work.
- Accelerating onboarding and knowledge transfer: A well-structured governance framework reduces the dependency on tribal knowledge. It makes it easier to onboard new staff or partners by providing clear documentation of KPIs, business rules, and data structures.
- Strengthening compliance and audit readiness: Centralized governance ensures data traceability, security, and quality policies are embedded from the start. This is particularly valuable for organizations operating in regulated environments, where audit trails and data governance are mandatory.
- Facilitating strategic prioritization: Mapping business initiatives to measurable goals makes it easier for executives to identify which projects contribute the most value. This helps prioritize investments and focus efforts where they will generate the highest return.
- Creating transparency and accountability: By explicitly assigning ownership of KPIs, business processes, and datasets, the framework clarifies responsibilities and fosters accountability across the organization. This reduces ambiguity and enables better governance of performance.

Solution-Level Benefits

Enhanced Quality

This approach significantly improves the overall quality of the BI solution, particularly in the following areas:

- Optimized Customer Experience (CX): The refined BI solution provides users with a seamless and intuitive experience, ensuring stakeholders can efficiently access relevant insights without unnecessary complexity.
- Controlled Data Quality: By emphasizing governance, this approach ensures that data is accurate, reliable, and consistently validated across the organization.
- Strengthened KPI Governance and Data Catalog: Clear governance policies for KPIs and data cataloging ensure consistency, making metrics and datasets easily understandable and actionable by all stakeholders.
- Increased Maintainability: The modular and well-documented design of the solution reduces technical debt, making future upgrades and maintenance efforts less costly and time-consuming.

Alignment with Organizational Goals

The approach ensures the BI solution is closely aligned with the organization's overall objectives, providing tangible value in the following ways:

- Portfolio Rationalization: The BI portfolio is streamlined to focus on high-value components, eliminating redundant or obsolete reports, dashboards, and processes.
- Consistency Across Stakeholders: A unified approach to data definitions and processes fosters alignment among diverse business units, reducing conflicts and miscommunication.
- Support for Organizational Objectives: By directly linking BI initiatives to strategic goals, the solution supports and accelerates the organization's broader objectives.

Project-Level Benefits

Portfolio Management Efficiency

Projects managed under this approach experience faster cycles, higher returns, and a focus on value, as demonstrated by:

- Reduced Time to Market: Streamlined processes and well-defined goals enable quicker project delivery, ensuring stakeholders receive actionable insights faster.
- Fail Fast for Low-Value Projects: The approach encourages the rapid identification of initiatives with low added value, allowing resources to be redirected to higher-priority projects.
- Maximized ROI: With a focus on aligning BI initiatives with strategic goals, resources are effectively allocated to projects with the highest potential impact.

Team Dynamics and Productivity

The structured methodology fosters a positive and productive environment for BI teams, resulting in:

- Reduced UAT Workload: Clearer requirements and better-aligned solutions reduce the need for exhaustive User Acceptance Testing (UAT), saving both time and effort.
- Improved Team Retention: A well-structured BI initiative, tied to impactful projects, motivates team members and fosters a sense of purpose, reducing turnover.
- Motivated and Proactive Teams: By involving the team in decision making and fostering ownership, the approach cultivates a motivated workforce capable of proposing innovative solutions and adapting to challenges.

By focusing on organizational solution and project-level benefits, this approach not only enhances technical quality and alignment with organizational goals but also ensures efficient project management and engaged teams, making it a holistic and effective methodology for BI initiatives.

High-Level Overview

The following framework outlines five key stages, detailing the types of information collected and the corresponding technical design layers applied at each step. This structured approach ensures both a comprehensive and logical process for building BI solutions.

Each of the five steps captures distinct yet interdependent layers of insight, forming a bridge between business understanding and technical implementation.

1. Business Goals

   The first step in achieving effective BI governance is to clearly articulate the organization's strategic goals. These high-level objectives should be collected through engagement with senior leadership and departmental heads to ensure alignment with the broader mission of the organization. At this stage, the business analyst facilitates conversations that define not just what the organization is aiming to achieve, but also why these goals matter. This alignment provides the foundation for the entire BI architecture, ensuring all subsequent designs serve a unified direction.

2. Key Results

   Once the strategic objectives are defined, the next step involves identifying the expected, measurable outcomes that indicate whether these objectives are being met. These outcomes, or key results, must be precise, quantifiable, and closely linked to the strategic goals. To support this, KPIs and data catalogs are created. KPIs translate abstract goals into tangible metrics, while data catalogs ensure that the underlying data is well documented, accessible, and standardized. This step requires the involvement of middle management and process owners, who provide operational insight into what success looks like and how it should be tracked. By clearly defining key results, organizations promote accountability, enable performance monitoring, and ensure transparent decision making across teams.

3. Business Events

   With goals and KPIs clarified, attention turns to understanding the core business activities that generate the data used in decision making. This involves identifying the main activities and events within each functional area that are relevant to the objectives. These processes are formalized using business process modeling techniques and are then supported by a centralized data warehouse. The data warehouse integrates disparate sources and serves as a unified platform for storing and analyzing business event data. This design not only supports daily operational reporting but also enables strategic analytics by offering a holistic view of the organization's functioning.

4. Business Concepts

At this stage, the business analyst works closely with functional stakeholders and the MDM team to clarify and formalize business concepts. These are the terms and definitions used across departments that need to be standardized to ensure consistent interpretation. This information is captured in a data dictionary, which becomes the reference for both business users and technical teams. A shared vocabulary reduces misunderstandings, enhances collaboration, and improves the accuracy of reporting and analytics. Achieving consensus on terminology can be politically sensitive, especially in large organizations, but it is essential for governance. In some cases, old and new definitions may need to coexist during transition periods to ensure business continuity.

5. Operational Data

Finally, the technical foundation of the BI solution is completed by identifying and integrating the relevant operational databases. These are the systems that hold transactional or raw data reflecting real-world business activities. The business analyst, often in collaboration with data engineers and IT architects, ensures that these sources meet the quality, completeness, and timeliness requirements needed to support the KPIs and reporting infrastructure. This step confirms that the BI system is grounded in reliable, accurate data, which is essential for informed decision making and sustainable performance monitoring (Figure 4.8).

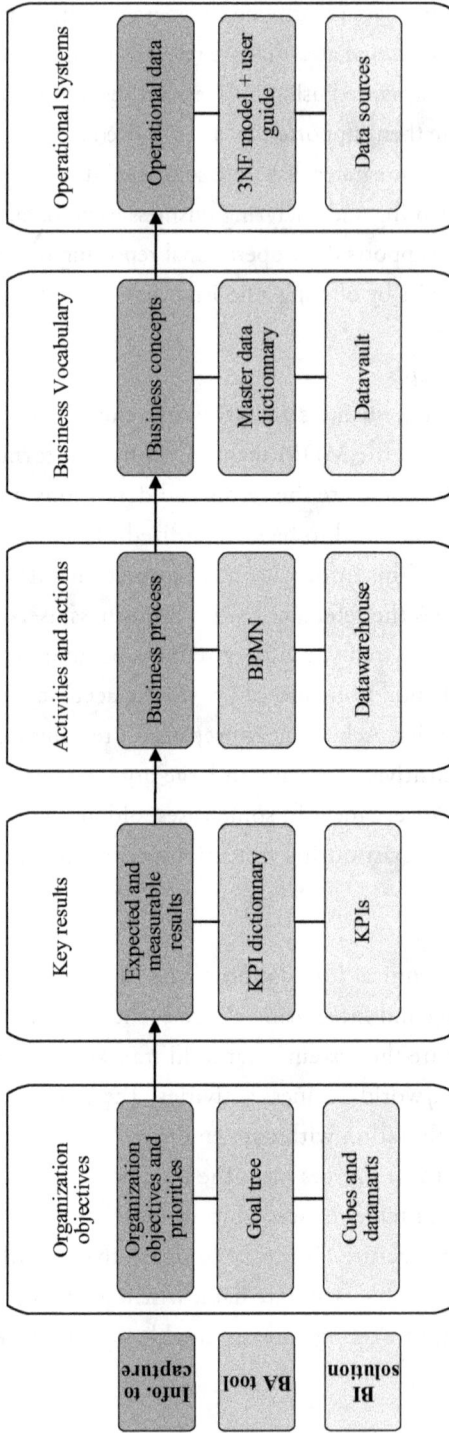

Figure 4.8 Framework for BI project approach

Example

This example will serve to illustrate the entire chapter through a comprehensive and concrete scenario. As the CEO of Zonama, an online marketplace offering a broad range of product categories, I have set the objective to enhance the customer experience by "delivering a world-class, frictionless, and trusted customer journey." To achieve this, I will engage with each business department to gather their input on how their respective areas can contribute to this goal. Ultimately, the outcome of this initiative will be the development of a consolidated dashboard that enables the organization to monitor and manage customer experience across all business functions.

Detailed Steps to Achieve BI Governance

With the overall framework in place, the next section walks through each step in detail, translating the structure into concrete, actionable steps. Each step identifies the key conversations to have, the stakeholders who hold essential information, and the technical outputs to be designed. By mixing individual and group discussions, this approach ensures that every perspective is heard—from strategic objectives to operational realities—while progressively shaping a shared foundation for the BI solution.

Understanding the Objectives

Begin by gathering the business and stakeholder objectives through discussions with the sponsor and users. The initial focus is on identifying and understanding the business problem that the solution will address. These objectives can be formalized using several frameworks, such as a goal tree, SMART/ER (Specific, Measureable, Attainable, Relevant, Timely, Evaluative/Ethical, and Rewarding) goals, the COBIT (Control Objectives for Information and Related Technologies) framework, or OKR (Objectives and Key Results) framework.

Among these, the goal tree is often the most straightforward and effective approach. This method uses a hierarchical visualization to break down strategic objectives into tactical and operational ones. A weighting method can be applied to prioritize goals and ensure alignment with organizational strategy.

The Role of the Goal Tree

A goal tree provides a structured way to document the rationale behind the business need for a solution, linking each component to the company strategy. This visualization captures:

- Strategic Objectives: High-level goals aligned with the overall organizational mission
- Tactical Objectives: Intermediate goals that bridge the gap between strategy and operations
- Operational Objectives: Specific actions required to achieve tactical and strategic goals

For example, a product delivery service goal tree might show how improving delivery times (a strategic goal) cascades into specific actions like optimizing warehouse logistics (tactical) and streamlining order tracking systems (operational) (Figure 4.9).

In this step, the CEO defines the overall objective and works with each department to identify subgoals or specific actions that contribute to achieving it. Each department takes ownership of its assigned subgoal. The CEO then assigns a priority to each subgoal, reflecting the extent to which it contributes to the main objective. While a goal tree can include multiple layers of goals, this example is limited to two layers for the sake of clarity and simplicity.

Why This Step Matters

Using a goals tree or a similar approach offers numerous benefits:

- Consistency Across the Solution: It ensures everyone understands the business challenges and objectives, helping to align priorities with stakeholder expectations rather than purely technical constraints.

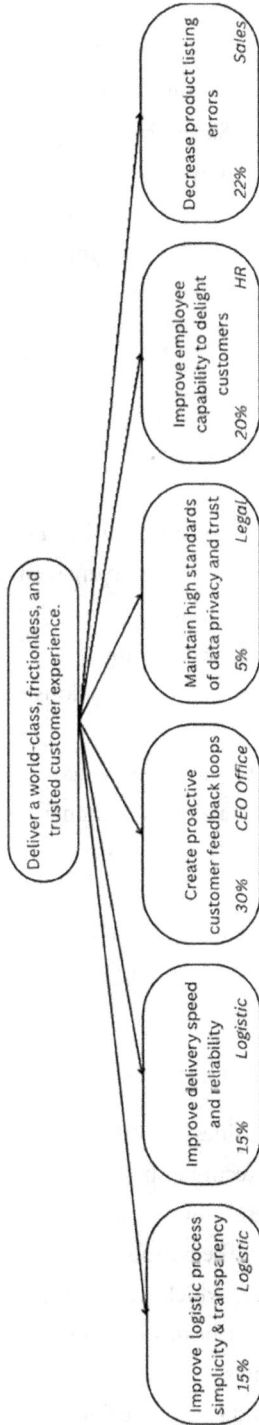

Figure 4.9 Example of Zonama goal tree

- Objective-Driven Prioritization: Instead of basing priorities on project or technical requirements alone, the process is guided by stakeholder objectives, minimizing inconsistencies.
- Change Management Support: Linking objectives to developments ensures that changes in scope can only occur when justified by shifts in strategy or the functional domain. This reduces unnecessary revisions driven by changing stakeholders or personal agendas.

When This Step Is Critical

This step is particularly essential when:

1. Strategic Alignment Is Key: It establishes a direct connection between the BI solution and the company strategy, ensuring the system remains relevant and usable.
2. Frequent Changes Are Likely: By justifying scope changes with strategic reasons, this step prevents disruptions caused by unwarranted priority shifts and scope creep.
3. Stakeholder Turnover Occurs: The structured approach provides continuity, even when stakeholders change, as the objectives remain the focal point.

This alignment helps maintain team motivation by avoiding demoralizing, unclear changes, and by providing a clear rationale for adjustments.

Stakeholder Conversations and Ownership

At this initial stage, the business analyst engages primarily with senior stakeholders, such as the executive sponsor, department heads, and strategic decision makers. These individuals hold the vision and set the organization's key objectives. Their input is crucial to understanding the "why" behind the initiative, which helps frame the overall purpose of the BI project. Each of them brings their own perspective and strategic priorities. The business analyst's role is to collect these viewpoints, translate them into clear goals, and facilitate prioritization. These conversations are generally individual, providing space for candid expression of needs and expectations. Ownership of this information lies with those responsible for the organization's strategic direction.

Key Results

Once the objectives are clearly defined, the next step is to determine how to measure their success. This involves identifying and establishing the right metrics and KPIs to make the objectives actionable and measurable. Without appropriate indicators, it is impossible to gauge progress, evaluate success, or justify changes. This step directly translates high-level objectives into quantifiable results, ensuring alignment and accountability (Figure 4.10).

Why This Step Is Crucial

Defining key results is a mandatory step in the BI process. It provides clarity on what "success" looks like, enabling all stakeholders to work toward a common goal. This alignment ensures that everyone, from technical teams to business leaders, operates with the same understanding and uses consistent definitions for concepts and metrics.

However, this step can be challenging, as it often involves reconciling differing perspectives and priorities among stakeholders. Achieving consensus on a single definition for each concept can be politically sensitive but is critical for ensuring effective communication and decision making. This alignment process often begins by presenting the various technical definitions of a given concept to the business stakeholders and facilitating a structured discussion around them. The goal is to agree on a shared measures that accurately reflects business meaning while remaining implementable in technical systems. When consensus is difficult to reach, it may be necessary to escalate the issue to higher levels of management to ensure alignment with strategic priorities. In some cases, legacy definitions may need to be retired if they hinder clarity or impede transformation efforts. However, to ease the transition, both the old and new definitions can coexist temporarily, allowing teams to adapt gradually while maintaining continuity. When done correctly, this step allows everyone to speak the same "language," minimizing confusion and misinterpretation.

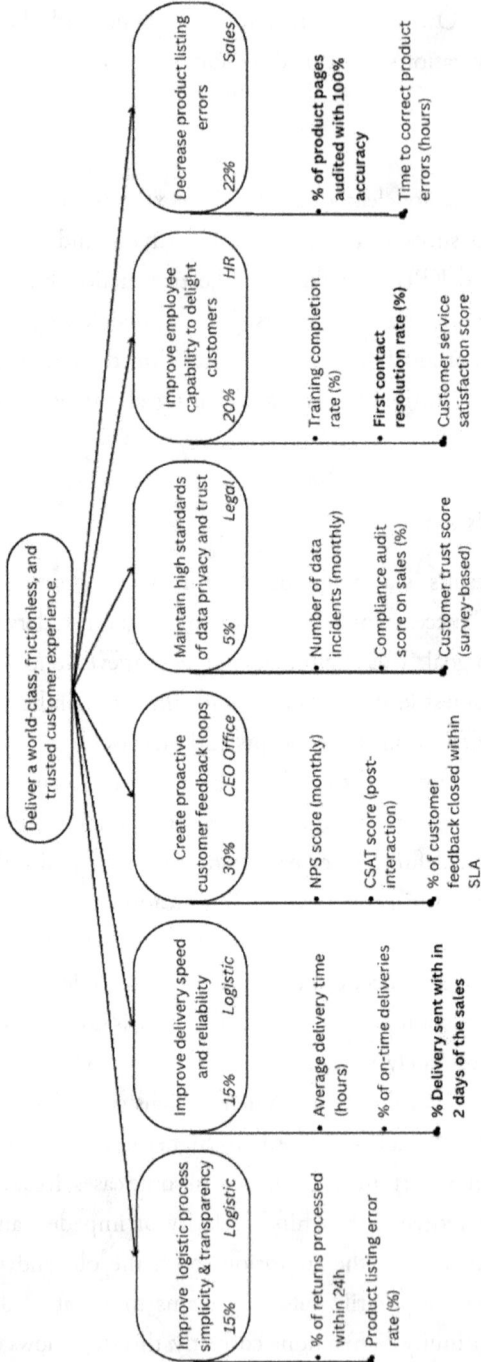

Figure 4.10 Example of Zonama with KPIs

When Is This Step Critical?

This step is vital in every BI initiative, but it becomes particularly critical in the following situations:

- High-Stakes Reporting: When reports are presented to top management, any misalignment in metrics or definitions can lead to misleading insights and erroneous decisions.
- Cross-Departmental Collaboration: When multiple departments rely on the same BI system, consistent definitions are crucial to avoid conflicts or discrepancies in reporting.
- Strategic Decision Making: When KPIs are tied to organizational strategy, clear alignment ensures that BI efforts support long-term goals.

Practical Application of Key Results

Once the metrics are defined, they can be utilized by various teams to ensure alignment and delivery:

- For Developers: These definitions guide the creation of indicators, cubes, and visualizations. Developers can use the agreed-upon KPIs as a foundation for designing accurate and consistent dashboards, reports, and analytics tools.
- For Business Analysts: Analysts can address stakeholders separately to identify differences in priorities, find common ground, and ensure that all metrics meet user expectations. This dialogue also helps to bridge gaps between technical and functional teams.

Maximizing Value

A comprehensive global list of KPIs serves several purposes:

- Facilitating Conversations Across Teams: A shared understanding of what success means fosters collaboration and ensures consistency in reporting and analysis.
- Providing a Clear Overview for C-Level Executives: Consolidated KPIs offer a high-level view of business performance, making it easier for senior management to monitor progress and make informed decisions.

- Enhancing Business Activity Mastery: Including KPIs for data quality or metrics defined using the thermometer method can add significant value. These KPIs can provide quick, actionable insights into business operations with minimal additional effort.

Data Quality KPIs

Data quality KPIs should always align with the goals outlined during the objective-setting phase. These indicators help assess whether the data is sufficient to support the business goals and provide a clear go/no-go criterion for the project.

For example:

- If the data quality is inadequate to achieve the business objectives, it may be more effective to delay the BI project or revisit the data collection and management processes. Sometime aborting it is the best option,
- By establishing minimum thresholds for data quality, stakeholders can ensure that resources are not wasted on building systems that cannot deliver meaningful insights. More examples of setting thresholds are available in Chapter 3, Data Quality and Thermometers sections.

Key Takeaways

Defining key results ensures that BI efforts remain focused and effective. It provides a shared framework for evaluating success, facilitates better communication across departments, and aligns BI initiatives with organizational priorities. By incorporating well-defined metrics and data quality criteria, the BI system becomes a powerful tool for driving informed decision making and maximizing value across the organization.

Stakeholder Conversations and Ownership

This step requires engaging both middle management and the business process owner. Middle managers are best positioned to articulate operational goals and translate strategic directions into measurable outcomes. The business process owner brings in-depth knowledge of day-to-day activities and helps validate that the KPIs selected are not only aligned with objectives but also grounded in the reality of how the process works.

The business analyst plays a crucial role in facilitating this conversation to ensure the list of KPIs is comprehensive and unambiguous. This means building a KPI dictionary that avoids confusion—making sure each term has a single, agreed-upon definition and preventing situations where one KPI name refers to different calculations depending on the team. This structured dialogue is essential for establishing a shared understanding of success, minimizing misinterpretations, and laying a consistent foundation for both analysis and communication across the organization.

Business Events

After defining the goals and metrics, the next critical step is to understand the business processes that need monitoring. This is often formalized using BPMN (Business Process Model and Notation)-like model. BPMN is a standardized graphical representation of business processes that facilitates communication among stakeholders, including both technical and nontechnical teams. Its intuitive notation provides a clear view of activities, roles, and sequences, making it an essential tool for modeling processes within a BI framework.

Overview of BPMN

BPMN is widely used to capture and communicate business processes due to its clarity and flexibility. It employs flowchart-like diagrams, using a set of standardized elements such as events (start, intermediate, and end), activities (tasks or subprocesses), gateways (decision points), and connectors (sequences or message flows). These elements enable teams to document complex processes in a structured yet accessible format. By using BPMN, organizations can:

1. Visualize the entire process to monitor from start to finish.
2. Identify key business events and activities that need monitoring.
3. Highlight inefficiencies, redundancies, or gaps in the process.
4. Facilitate conversations between technical and functional stakeholders by providing a common language.

For example, a BPMN model can show how sales orders are processed, from receiving a customer order to delivering the product, including intermediate steps such as inventory checks and payment confirmation. This ensures alignment between stakeholders and helps pinpoint events where data needs to be captured. It highlights the link between events and business goals. The business event or piece of work is getting priority because it has more value for the company (supporting more goals) than any other pieces of work (Figure 4.11).

A business event refers to a real-world occurrence or transaction that is meaningful to the organization—such as a sale, a customer registration, or a product return. In BI and data warehousing, these events are systematically translated into fact tables to support analysis and reporting. Here's how this translation works:

1. Identifying the Event of Interest
   First, the business analyst determines which event to monitor based on the business goals and KPIs. For example, in an e-commerce company, a "customer purchase" is a key event that aligns with revenue tracking or customer behavior analysis.

2. Defining the Grain (Level of Detail)
   Next, the grain of the fact table is defined. This refers to the exact level at which the event is captured—for example, "one row per product sold per transaction" or "one row per completed order." This definition must be consistent to ensure clarity and comparability of data.

3. Capturing the Measurements
   The fact table stores quantitative metrics related to the event—such as sales amount, quantity, discount, tax, or processing time. These are the "facts" that will be aggregated and analyzed.

4. Linking to Dimensions
   To make the event meaningful in context, the fact table is linked to multiple dimension tables. These dimensions provide descriptive information about the event—such as:
   ○ Customer dimension: Who made the purchase?
   ○ Time dimension: When did the purchase occur?
   ○ Product dimension: What was purchased?
   ○ Channel dimension: Where or how was the order placed?

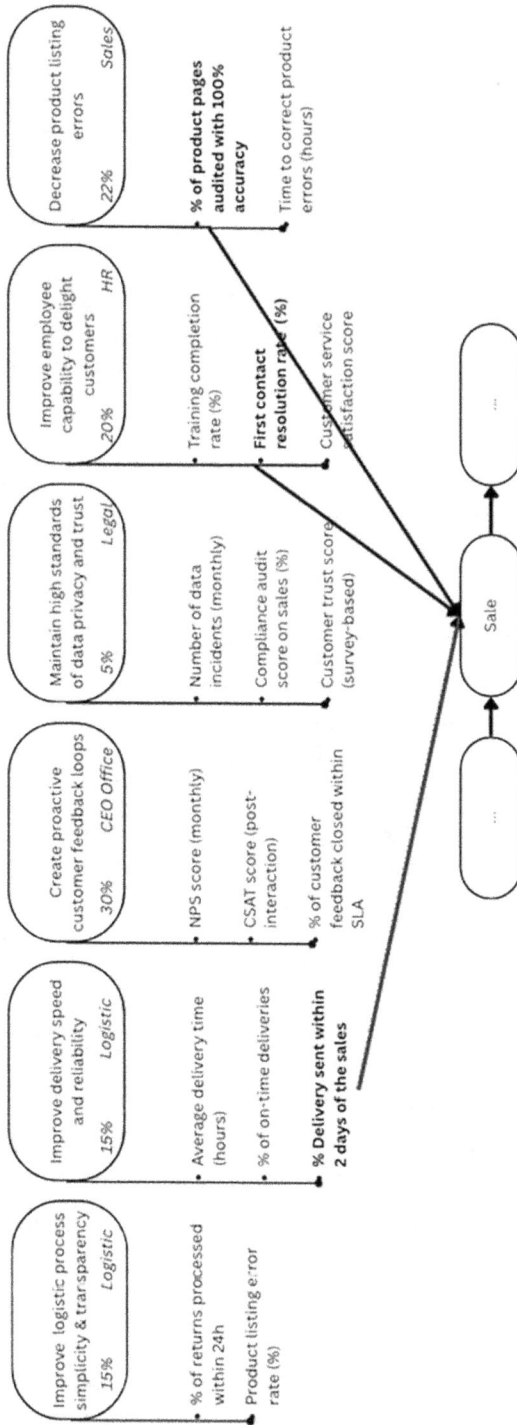

Figure 4.11 Link between the business process and the business objectives

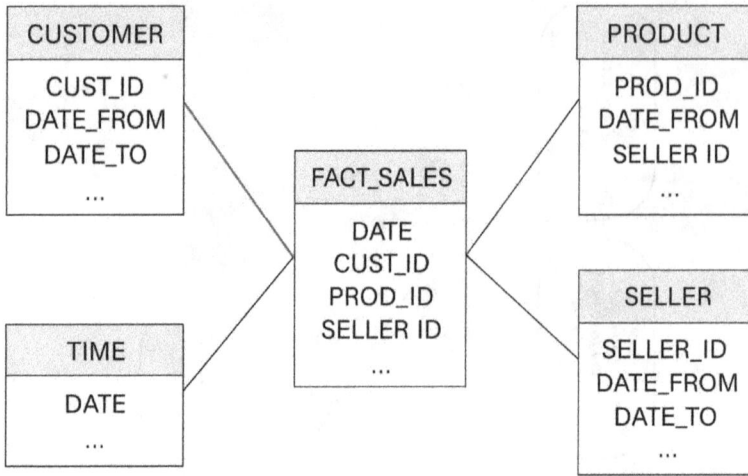

Figure 4.12 Fact table of the business process

5. Ensuring Referential Integrity and Integration

Fact tables are integrated with master data and transactional systems to ensure consistency and completeness. The business analyst works with data engineers to confirm that all relevant data sources are aligned with the business definitions (Figure 4.12).

Why Is This Step Helpful?

Creating a BPMN diagram offers a graphical representation of business activities, making it easier to visualize what needs to be monitored. It provides an intuitive overview of workflows and how different activities relate to business goals. This step is especially useful for understanding:

- The critical business events or "facts" that drive the process
- Points in the process where data is generated or transformed
- Opportunities to improve efficiency or streamline operations

Importantly, it's crucial to model processes according to the business goals. Not all steps in a process need to be documented initially—only those that are relevant to achieving the stakeholders' objectives. Additional steps or subprocesses can be modeled in later iterations, ensuring the development effort is focused on high-priority areas.

When Is This Step Critical?

This step is particularly important in the following scenarios:

- When Processes Are Not Well Controlled: If the business process is not under control or data does not comply with it, modeling the process helps identify root causes and discrepancies.
- When Stakeholder Alignment Is Lacking: BPMN serves as a powerful conversation starter among stakeholders. It provides a visual framework for agreeing on organizational objectives and definitions of success.
- When Defining Data Sources: Understanding business events and processes ensures that the right data sources are identified and integrated into the BI solution.

Without agreement on the modeled process, stakeholders may have conflicting views of the organization's objectives and definitions of success.

What to Do with This Information

The business events defined in the BPMN-like model become the foundation of the BI system's data model. Typically, these events are represented as fact tables in a Kimball's star schema. The developer must carefully consider the grain (level of detail) of these events. If the grain is inconsistent, it can highlight limitations or inefficiencies in the solution (it might be required to complete or investigate other sources).

Additionally, the BPMN model provides a common ground for identifying data sources and understanding how they align with business processes. This is particularly useful when dealing with evolving or "protean" processes that may change frequently.

Maximizing Value

- Focus on What Matters: Model only the parts of the process directly related to the defined objectives. This ensures development efforts are aligned with business priorities and avoids wasting resources on unnecessary details.
- Compare Model to Data Behavior: By comparing the BPMN model to actual data behavior, the business analyst can identify discrepancies between stakeholders' understanding of processes and the reality. This comparison highlights areas needing attention, such as data quality issues or process inefficiencies.
- Prioritize Developments: The BPMN model provides a roadmap for prioritizing development efforts. Steps in the process that deliver the most significant value to business priorities should be addressed first. Since this layer often represents the largest development effort, efficient prioritization is critical.

By integrating business processes into the BI strategy through BPMN, organizations can ensure their solutions are aligned with real-world activities, effectively monitored, and capable of supporting high-priority business goals.

Stakeholder Conversations and Ownership

At this stage, the business analyst needs to work closely with the business process owner, who is typically the most knowledgeable about how the process unfolds in real life. This individual can articulate the key events that trigger actions and decisions, which are essential to model the right business events for monitoring and reporting.

It is equally important for the business analyst to ensure that this person maintains a holistic view of all possible scenarios—not just the ideal or most common workflows. Oversight of edge cases, exceptions, or less frequent events can result in critical gaps in the data model. Encouraging this broader perspective helps build a solution that reflects the true complexity of the business process and avoids overlooking data patterns that may carry significant business value. At the same time, the business analyst must strike a careful balance: while it is essential to capture a comprehensive view, they must also avoid becoming entangled in excessive detail related to data quality anomalies, rare edge cases, or outdated historical process variations. Not every scenario requires immediate modeling, and discerning where to draw the line ensures the analysis remains both efficient and actionable. This pragmatic approach supports a more resilient design for the underlying data warehouse and ensures that the BI system remains accurate, scalable, and relevant over time.

Business Concepts

At this stage, the business analyst collaborates with stakeholders to establish consensus on key business concepts. This alignment is crucial because these concepts will define the axes for analyzing data, ensuring that all parties operate with a shared understanding. A unified approach can be achieved through tools like a common glossary or methodologies such as the ELM.

Ensemble Logical Model

The ELM (see Chapter 3, Ensemble Logical Model section) method is designed to harmonize terminologies and relationships across stakeholders, providing a structured way to establish clarity. By identifying entities, their attributes, and the relationships between them, ELM helps create a framework for defining and agreeing on business concepts. This model works as follows:

1. Entity Identification: Define the core business entities relevant to the stakeholders, such as products, customers, sales, transactions, or regions.
2. Attributes Specification: Clarify the attributes that describe each entity. For instance, a customer might have attributes like name, address, segment.
3. Relationship Mapping: Establish how these entities relate to one another. For example, a product is purchased by a customer, or a transaction occurs in a specific region.
4. Unified Glossary: Consolidate the findings into a shared glossary, ensuring every stakeholder uses standardized terms.

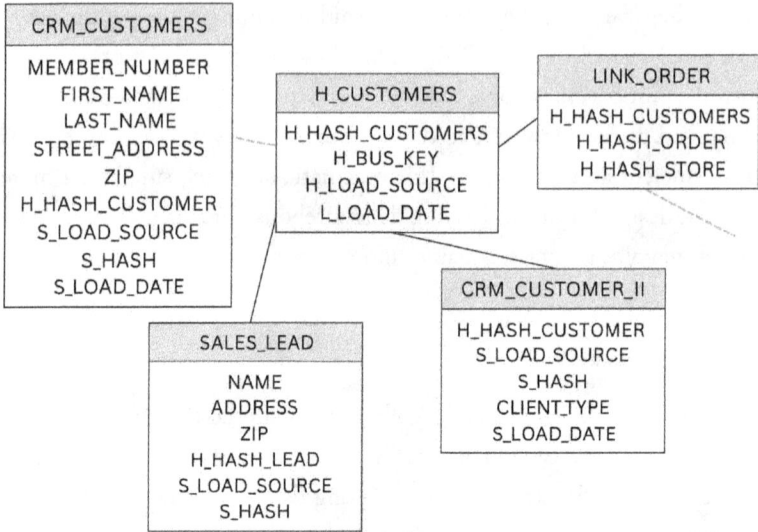

CRM_CUSTOMERS

MEMBER_NUMBER
FIRST_NAME
LAST_NAME
STREET_ADDRESS
ZIP
H_HASH_CUSTOMER
S_LOAD_SOURCE
S_HASH
S_LOAD_DATE

H_CUSTOMERS

H_HASH_CUSTOMERS
H_BUS_KEY
H_LOAD_SOURCE
L_LOAD_DATE

LINK_ORDER

H_HASH_CUSTOMERS
H_HASH_ORDER
H_HASH_STORE

SALES_LEAD

NAME
ADDRESS
ZIP
H_HASH_LEAD
S_LOAD_SOURCE
S_HASH

CRM_CUSTOMER_II

H_HASH_CUSTOMER
S_LOAD_SOURCE
S_HASH
CLIENT_TYPE
S_LOAD_DATE

Figure 4.13 EML model of the customer business concept

ELM ensures that ambiguities in business language are minimized, fostering alignment and supporting downstream data modeling (Figure 4.13).

Why Is This Step Helpful?

The alignment of business concepts can range from being a simple formality to a labor-intensive process, depending on the organization's size and complexity. Its purpose is to ensure that stakeholders use clear, meaningful, and standardized concepts. In large organizations with diverse departments, this step can be challenging but is essential for achieving consistency.

By addressing this step effectively, the organization reduces misunderstandings, misinterpretations, and discrepancies in data usage. It lays the foundation for building robust analytical tools and enhances collaboration across teams.

When Is This Step Critical?

This step becomes indispensable in large, complex organizations where multiple stakeholders need to collaborate and share insights. For effective communication and consistent decision making, stakeholders must share common business concepts and perspectives. This ensures that reports, analyses, and dashboards are based on universally understood terms and frameworks.

What to Do with This Information

The agreed-upon business concepts serve multiple purposes:

1. Creation of Common Dimensions and Filters: These concepts inform the development of analytical dimensions and filters, which enable users to slice and dice data consistently.
2. Foundation for Data Modeling: Business concepts can form the basis of a Data Vault layer, which stores all historized business concepts. This layer acts as the root for building a Kimball-style Data Warehouse, providing reusable building blocks for the organization's analytical framework.

For example, if "customer" is a core business concept, its definition and attributes (e.g., name, segment, and lifetime value) will guide how customer-related data is stored, historized, and analyzed across different systems.

Maximizing Value

Given that aligning on business concepts can be time-consuming, it's important to focus on core business concepts and dimensions. A pragmatic approach is to leverage the business keys and grains identified in the previous step (Business Events) and derive the main axes and concepts from them. This ensures that only the most critical elements are addressed initially, delivering immediate value while keeping efforts manageable.

By focusing on core concepts and ensuring they are integrated into a reusable data layer, organizations can achieve both short-term analytical capabilities and a sustainable foundation for future growth.

Stakeholder Conversations and Ownership

Clarifying business concepts requires the business analyst to engage with cross-functional business stakeholders, especially middle management, who can articulate the core terms, labels, and dimensions used within their domains. These conversations help ensure that all parties are referring to the same concepts in the same way—whether discussing a "customer," a "product," or a "sale."

In organizations with established MDM teams, these stakeholders play a pivotal role in validating definitions and ensuring consistency across systems. The MDM team is typically responsible for maintaining a single, authoritative version of key business entities, and their input is crucial to align business concepts across departments and reporting systems.

This step is particularly important in large organizations, where the same term may carry different meanings in different contexts. The business analyst's role is to identify and resolve semantic ambiguities—whether caused by synonyms (two words for the same concept) or polysemy (the same word used for different concepts). Ensuring clarity at this stage will strengthen the quality of reporting, improve communication across teams, and lay a solid foundation for analytics.

Operational Data

The BI business analyst plays a crucial role in identifying and understanding the data sources tied to the business processes. This involves locating the relevant data within operational systems, which serve as a trace of business activities. The analyst must evaluate whether these data sources are suitable to achieve the business objectives by assessing their quality, historical retention, latency, and completeness in relation to the business processes being monitored.

In this step, the analyst also quantifies the percentage of data completeness to ensure that the dataset adequately represents the business process. By doing so, the analyst determines whether the data is sufficient to support the BI objectives and whether it meets the defined requirements and a go/no go project (Figure 4.14).

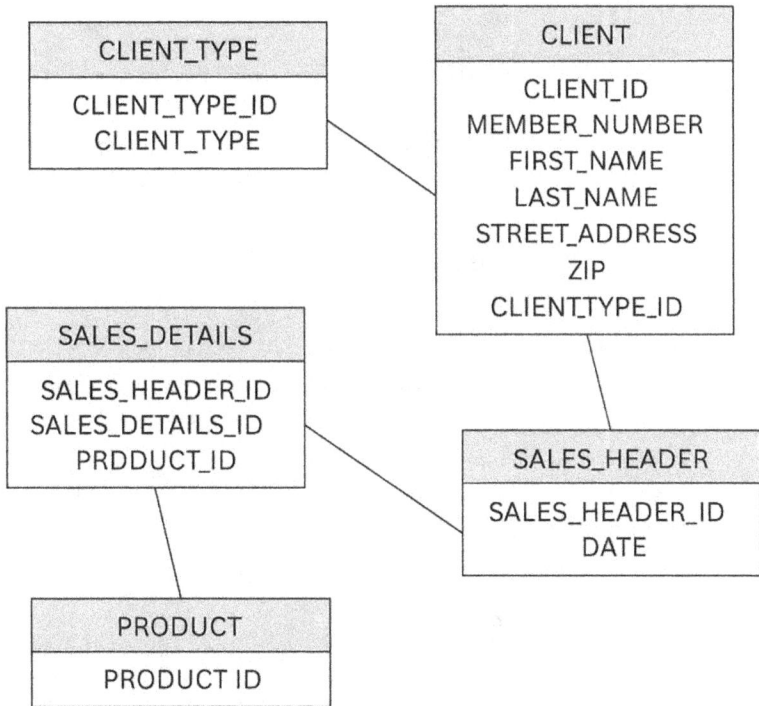

Figure 4.14 Zonama operational database schema chunk

At this stage, the design of the operational databases supporting Zonama's sales is used to document the data sources that will feed the system being developed.

Why Is This Step Helpful?

This step is invaluable for developers, as it provides the foundational understanding required to manipulate and integrate data effectively. Without a clear picture of how the data is structured, accessed, and aligned with business needs, creating a robust BI solution is impossible. It bridges the gap between business concepts and technical implementation, ensuring that data integration aligns with business objectives.

Moreover, this step supports the establishment of data quality KPIs, ensuring that any issues or discrepancies can be measured and addressed systematically.

When Is This Step Critical?

This step becomes particularly critical in the following scenarios:

- Multiple Data Sources: When a business process involves several data sources, integration becomes complex, and ensuring consistency across these sources is vital.
- Low-Quality Data: If data quality is subpar, extra effort is needed to clean and validate the data to avoid inaccurate insights.
- Long Historical Data Requirements: When the project requires extensive historical data, understanding the evolution of operational data rules and business events over time is essential.

Failing to address these complexities upfront can lead to significant challenges in the later stages of the project.

What to Do with This Information

The information gathered during this step is instrumental for developers as they integrate data sources into the BI solution. It guides the transformation, cleaning, and loading processes, ensuring that the data is ready for analysis. Additionally, this information often helps define data quality KPIs, which are used to monitor and maintain the integrity of the data over time.

At this stage, the concepts, models, and plans developed earlier are brought into alignment with the actual data. This step frequently reveals discrepancies between theoretical definitions and practical realities, enabling the team to identify and address gaps in business concepts or processes.

Maximizing Value

To maximize value and avoid unnecessary delays, it is crucial to involve stakeholders early and maintain open communication. Discrepancies between datasets and predefined concepts can stem from various issues, such as:

- Poorly defined business concepts
- False assumptions by stakeholders or analysts
- Changes in business processes over time
- Data entry errors or loading issues

By proactively addressing these issues and collaborating with stake-holders, the team can minimize rework and reduce time-consuming trou-bleshooting. Developers can focus on delivering a BI solution that reflects the actual business processes, ensuring that insights derived from the data are accurate and actionable.

Stakeholder Conversations and Ownership

The final step involves working with the technical data owners, includ-ing data engineers, system administrators, and application managers who manage the source systems. These are the people who understand where data lives, how it is collected, and what limitations exist in terms of avail-ability, quality, history, and latency. The analyst needs to validate whether the identified business events and KPIs can actually be supported by exist-ing data. This may require source system audits or data profiling exercises. Ownership of this information is technical, but the analyst plays a key role in assessing alignment with business expectations. This step often reveals data gaps or discrepancies, enabling early corrective actions and avoiding downstream surprises.

Extra Step: Addressing User Emotions

A preliminary step, still being explored and refined at the time of writ-ing, offers a unique approach to understanding the user's perspective. This step focuses on neuroscience and addressing the emotions and daily challenges of stakeholders, acknowledging that everyone ulti-mately shares the same goal: "having a good day with minimal stress or drama."

The business analyst can start the project by asking insightful and empathetic questions, such as:

- "What does a bad day look like for you?"
- "What could happen that immediately tells you there's no time for coffee today?"
- "It's 9 a.m., and you already know you need to cancel dinner plans—what happened?"

Why Are These Questions Powerful?

These questions are effective for several reasons:

1. Shifting Focus to Business Problems: By framing the conversation around real-world pain points, the discussion remains grounded in identifying business challenges rather than jumping prematurely into solutions. This prevents stakeholders from proposing solutions that may not address the root cause.
2. Highlighting Priorities: Such questions help quickly pinpoint critical areas that cause disruptions or stress in the users' day-to-day operations. These pain points often represent high-priority issues that need to be monitored and resolved.
3. This approach signals that the analyst genuinely values the stakeholders' perspectives and experiences, helping to build trust and encourage open dialogue. When stakeholders feel heard and respected, they are more likely to engage actively and take ownership of the project. It also shows that the analyst is committed to supporting their needs beyond simply delivering a tool—demonstrating a broader, people-centered commitment to success.

How Does This Help the Process?

- Prioritization: Understanding what constitutes a "bad day" provides clear insights into which business processes or metrics should be prioritized in the BI solution.
- Early Alignment: These conversations help align the BI objectives with real-world scenarios, ensuring the solution is relevant and impactful.
- Avoiding Tunnel Vision: By steering the discussion toward problems rather than jumping to technical or superficial solutions, this step ensures a deeper understanding of the underlying issues.

Practical Outcomes

From these conversations, the business analyst can extract key insights into what needs to be monitored and addressed in the BI framework. For example:

- Identifying specific KPIs that stakeholders rely on to prevent "bad days"
- Highlighting critical business events that signal emerging problems
- Ensuring the BI solution proactively addresses user concerns, reducing stress and improving workflows

Conclusion

While still under research, this preliminary step offers significant potential to enhance the BI process by focusing on the human aspect of BI. By asking thoughtful, emotion-driven questions, the business analyst can uncover deeper insights, prioritize effectively, and create a solution that resonates with users' real needs. This empathetic approach not only builds better BI systems but also fosters stronger relationships between stakeholders and the project team.

Conclusion: Bringing It All Together—Strategy, Structure, and Empathy

The five-step framework presented in this chapter offers a clear, structured approach to building BI solutions that are not only technically sound but also strategically aligned and sustainable. Each step—defining objectives, identifying key results, modeling business events, clarifying business concepts, and grounding them in operational data—represents a vital link in the chain from business need to BI implementation.

What distinguishes this framework is its dual-dialogue structure: it promotes focused individual conversations with key stakeholders, while also encouraging cross-functional alignment through structured group sessions. This duality not only strengthens technical design through precise inputs but also helps navigate the political dimensions of organizational life, ensuring that divergent views are heard and harmonized.

But beyond processes and platforms, successful BI is also a human endeavor. That's why we introduced an optional yet powerful extra step—managing stakeholder emotions. By starting with simple, empathetic questions like, "What does a bad day look like?" or "When do you feel you're flying blind?" the business analyst uncovers the real pain points that often remain hidden behind formal requirements. This emotional insight gives substance to priorities and urgency to change, building trust and creating space for open, productive collaboration.

In the end, this framework is more than a method. It is a bridge between business vision and data execution, between people and platforms, between what matters and what is measurable. It equips the business analyst with a repeatable, scalable model—one that brings clarity to complexity and paves the way for high-impact, human-centered BI.

Bibliography

Al Neimat, Taimour. 2005. "Why IT Projects Fail." https://www.projectperfect .com.au/downloads/Info/info_it_projects_fail.pdf.

Aurum, Aybuke, and Claes Wohlin, eds. 2005. *Engineering and Managing Software Requirements*. Springer.

Bell, T. E., and T. A. Thayer. 1976. "Software Requirements: Are They Really a Problem?" Presented at the Proceedings of the 2nd International Conference on Software Engineering, San Francisco, October 13–15, 1976:61–68.

Biffl, Stefan, Aybuke Aurum, Barry Boehm, Hakan Erdogmus, and Paul Grundbücher. 2006. *Value-Based Software Engineering*. Springer.

Blokdyk, Gerardus. 2021. *Reporting and Business Intelligence—Standard Requirements*. 5STARCooks

Boehm, Barry W., and Philip N. Papaccio. 1988. "Understanding and Controlling Software Costs," *IEEE Transactions on Software Engineering* 14 (10): 1462–1477.

Brooks, F. P. 1987. "No Silver Bullet: Essence and Accidents of Software Engineering." *IEEE Computer* 20 (4): 10–19.

Bubenko, J., and J. Stirna. 1997. *EKD User Guide*. ELEKTRA Project, Research Report.

CIO WaterCooler. 2017. "The Data Governance Survey 2017". https://www .ciowatercooler.co.uk/resources/DataGovernanceSurvey2017.pdf.

Edward, J., I. Coutts, and S. McLeod. 2000. "Support for System Evolution Though Separating Business and Technology Issues in a Banking System." Presented at the Proceedings of International Conference on Software Maintenance, San Jose, CA, October 11–14. 2000:271–276.

European Software Institute. 1996. "European User Survey Analysis." Report (USV_EUR 2.1). ESPITI Project.

Ferragu, Emmanuel. 2013. *Modélisation des systèmes d'information décisionnels: techniques de modélisation conceptuelle et relationnelle des entrepôts de données*. Vuibert.

Gallup. n.d. "The Cost of Bad Project Management." https://news.gallup.com /businessjournal/152429/cost-bad-project-management.aspx.

Geneca. 2011. "Why Do Software Projects Fail? Study Reports Up to 75% of Software Projects Will Fail." https://www.geneca.com/why-up-to-75 -of-software-projects-will-fail/.

Heath-Carpentier, Amy. 2022. *The Challenge of Complexity: Essays by Edgar Morin*. Liverpool University Press.

Jarke, Matthias. 1993. "Requirements Engineering: An Integrated View of Representation, Process, and Domain." https://link.springer.com/chapter/10.1007/3-540-57209-0_8.

Kaufmann, Daniel, and Shang-Jing Wei. 2000. "Does 'Grease Money' Speed Up the Wheels of Commerce? IMF Working Paper. Authorized for distribution by Vito Tanzi.

Kimball, Ralph, and Margy Ross. 2002. *The Data Warehouse Toolkit: The Definitive Guide to Dimensional Modelling*. John Wiley.

Kotonya, G., and I. Sommerville. 1998. *Requirements Engineering: Processes and Techniques*. John Wiley.

Lahrmann, Gerrit, Frederik Marx, Robert Winter, and Felix Wortmann. 2010. "Business Intelligence Maturity Models: An Overview." https://www.itais.org/proceedings/itais2010/pdf/066.pdf.

Lindvall, Mikael, and Kristian Sandahl. 1998. "How Well Do Experienced Software Developers Predict Software Change?" *Journal of Systems and Software* 43 (1): 19–27.

Loucopoulos, P., V. Kavakli, N. Prekas, C. Rolland, G. Grosz, and S. Nurcan. 1997. "Using the EKD Approach: The Modelling Component." ELEKTRA Project, Athena Deliverable.

Lutz, R. R. 1993. "Analyzing Software Requirements Errors in Safety-Critical, Embedded Systems." Presented at the First International IEEE Symposium on Requirements Engineering (RE'93), San Diego, January 4–6, 1993:126–133.

Mannion, Mike, and Barry Keepence. 1995. "SMART Requirements." https://www.researchgate.net/publication/2937339_SMART_requirements.

Morin, Edgar. 2008. *On Complexity (Advances in Systems Theory, Complexity, and the Human Sciences)*. Alfonso Montuori (Foreword). Hampton Press.

Morin, Edgar, and Laurent Bibard. n.d. "L'avenir de la décision: connaitre et agir en complexité." ESSEC pour Coursera. https://www.coursera.org/learn/lavenir-de-la-decision?msockid=3df730577ae76a0f36fc25547b8a6b3d.

National Technical Reports Library. 1956. "Symposium on Advanced Programming Methods for Digital Computers, Washington, D. C., Jun 28, 29, 1956, Under the Joint Sponsorship of Navy Mathematical Computing Advisory Panel and Office of Naval Research." https://ntrl.ntis.gov/NTRL/dashboard/searchResults/titleDetail/PB121670.xhtml.

Nurcan Selmin, Camille Salinesi, Carine Souveyet, and Jolita Ralyté. 2010. *Intentional Perspectives on Information Systems Engineering*. Springer.

Olson, Timothy G. 2005. "Successful Strategies to Improve Your Requirements." Presented at the NDIA 2005 Systems Engineering Conference, San Diego, CA, October 24–27.

Persson, Anne, and Janis Stirna, 2018. *Enterprise Modeling: Facilitating the Process and the People*. Springer.

PMI. 2014. "Requirements Management: A Core Competency for Project and Program Success." www.pmi.org/-/media/PDF/Knowledge%20Center/PMI -Pulse-Requirements-Management-In-Depth-Report.ashx.

Prat, N. "Goal Formalisation and Classification for Requirements Engineering." Presented at the Proceedings of the Third International Workshop on Requirements Engineering: Foundations of Software Quality (REFSQ'97), Barcelona, June 1997:145–156, 1997.

Project Management Institute, 2012. *A Guide to the Project Management Body of Knowledge (PMBOK® Guide).* –5th ed. Project Management Institute.

ProjectSmart. 2014. "The Standish Group Report—Chaos Report." https:// www.projectsmart.co.uk/white-papers/chaos-report.pdf.

Rajterič, Irena Hribar. 2010. "Overview of Business Intelligence Maturity Models." *Management* 150 (1): 47–67.

Rak, Katija, Zeljka Car, and Ignac Lovrek. 2019. "Effort Estimation Mode for Each Phase of Software Development Life Cycle." *Journal of Software: Evolution and Process* 31 (2): e2119. https://onlinelibrary.wiley.com/doi /full/10.1002/smr.2119?msockid=3df730577ae76a0f36fc25547b8a6b3d.

Robertson, Suzanne, and James Robertson. 2012. *Mastering the Requirements Process: Getting Requirements Right.* 3rd ed. Addison-Wesley.

Rolland, Colette. 2003. *Ingenierie Des Besoins: L'Approche L'Ecritoire.* CRI Université de Paris 1—Sorbonne.

Scuba School International. n.d. "Diver Stress & Rescue Class." https://www .divessi.com/en/advanced-training/scuba-diving/stress-and-rescue.

Shaaban, Essam, Yehia Helmy. Ayman Khedr, and Mona Nasr. 2012. "Business Intelligence Maturity Models: Toward New Integrated Model." https://www .researchgate.net/publication/236626074_Business_Intelligence_Maturity _Models_Toward_New_Integrated_Model.

Standish Group. n.d. "CHAOS Report." CHAOS Report Beyond Infinity (digital version) – The Standish Group.

The Standish Group. 1995. "Chaos." Standish Group Internal Report, http:// www.standishgroup.com/chaos.html.

TDWI. n.d. "2020 Global State of Enterprise Analytics." https://tdwi.org/white papers/2020/06/bi-all-microstrategy-global-state-of-enterprise-analytics.aspx.

University of Southern California. 2008. "Phase Distribution of Software Development Effort." https://dl.acm.org/doi/10.1145/1414004.1414016.

Van Lamsweerde, Alex. 2000. "Requirement Engineering in the Year 2000: A Research Perspective." Presented at the Proceeding of the 22nd International Conference on Software Engineering (ICSE'2000), Limerick, Ireland, June 09, 2000:5–19.

Wiegers, Karl E. 2001. "Inspecting Requirements." Weekly Column, July 30, https://www.stickyminds.com/article/inspecting-requirements.

Web Links

https://blog.csgsolutions.com/how-to-create-a-business-intelligence-strategy
-step-by-step.

https://cdn.sisense.com/wp-content/uploads/analytics_to_ML.png.

https://static.aminer.org/pdf/PDF/000/361/405/software_requirements_are
_they_really_a_problem.pdf.

https://www.altexsoft.com/blog/business/product-roadmap-key-features
-common-types-and-roadmap-building-tips/.

https://www.altexsoft.com/blog/business-intelligence-strategy/.

https://www.cio.com/article/274511/7-keys-to-a-successful-business-intelligence
-strategy.html.

https://www.finereport.com/en/bi-tools/bi-strategy.html#What_is_a_successful
_BI_strategy.

https://www.franceinter.fr/emissions/la-tete-au-carre/la-tete-au-carre-01-juin
-2016.

https://www.gartner.com/en/topics/data-and-analytics.

https://www.researchgate.net/publication/278714953_Requirements_Engineering
_for_Agile_Methods.

https://www.tableau.com/learn/articles/business-intelligence/successful-strategy.

https://www.techtarget.com/searchbusinessanalytics/tip/7-key-steps-to-deploy
-a-modern-business-intelligence-strategy.

https://www.techtarget.com/searchbusinessanalytics/Ultimate-guide-to-business
-intelligence-in-the-enterprise.

https://www.volere.org/templates/volere-requirements-specification-template/.

About the Authors

Eva Polini is a globally recognized business intelligence expert who, for the last 20 years, has worked with UNICEF and companies such as Peugeot and Disney. She is the author of *Business Intelligence: Le Recueil des Besoins—La Boîte à Outils du Business analyst* (*Business Intelligence: Requirement Management—the Business Analyst's Toolbox*) (2020). Her experience is coupled with two master's degrees in knowledge management and information and communication systems from Sorbonne University (Paris, France).

Eva has worked across borders and industries, including telecommunications, finance, and legal. In 2019, she led a team to help an Australian telecommunications company avoid a multimillion dollar fine and audit, which saved their license. She is a sought-after expert in the BI field and continues to work on high-impact projects.

Karina Ghozali is a senior data visualization professional who has worked in the telecommunications and retail industries, delivering best practice visualizations and self-service assets since 2018.

She is passionate about telling stories with data and helping others make informed decisions by providing guided insights. She has worked with corporations, such as Optus and Big W, helping them build scalable assets across their organizations.

Index